No Ordinary Move

Relocating Your Aging Parents

Barbara Z. Perman, Ph. D. and Jim Ballard

Bloomington, IN Milton Keynes, UK

authorHOUSE®

AuthorHouse™
1663 Liberty Drive, Suite 200
Bloomington, IN 47403
www.authorhouse.com
Phone: 1-800-839-8640

AuthorHouse™ UK Ltd.
500 Avebury Boulevard
Central Milton Keynes, MK9 2BE
www.authorhouse.co.uk
Phone: 08001974150

First published by AuthorHouse 12/21/2006

ISBN: 978-1-4259-7224-0 (sc)

Library of Congress Control Number: 2006910171

Printed in the United States of America
Bloomington, Indiana

This book is printed on acid-free paper.

This book is for all those
who are searching for
the feeling of home,
with the hope that
they may find it
within themselves.

Acknowledgements

We want to thank a number of friends and colleagues who took the time to read our manuscript, provide feedback, and give us warm support. These include Jayne Pearl, John Clayton, Barbara Roswell, Sydney Hirsch, Cathy Huett, Martha Lawrence, and Ken Blanchard.

Special thanks to Teresa Bragg whose generous and unflagging spirit provided an underpinning for this project. Barbara wishes to express heartfelt gratitude to her dear parents Edith and Paul Perman and to Henry Allen who has been like a father to her, for being open to "saging"* as well as aging.

Finally we acknowledge humbly that even though we wrote this book, we are clear that we only acted as agents. The book came through us.

*The term saging comes from the work of Rabbi Zalman Schachter- -Shalomi on Spiritual Eldering.

Introduction

This is no ordinary book, because this is no ordinary time. Never before has a population of seventy-eight million people had to come to terms with both their own aging and that of their parents. A silent, slow-moving earthquake is taking place in the lives of these adult children. Typical of their fast-moving generation, most ignore the early warning tremors. Then one day the phone rings, and they find themselves in crisis. True to their style of dealing with interruptions, many will go for a quick fix—put the folks in a home, stash their stuff in a dumpster, and get back to the fifty-yard dash they call their lives.

Such an abrupt approach produces a painful uprooting, but more importantly a missed opportunity. For each event in the continuing saga of adult children helping relocate their elders opens a doorway of possibility. Viewed and approached in the right way, an event most would see as daunting or overwhelming becomes a sharing of wisdom across generations of different orientations and the expression of a love that has perhaps long lain unrealized and unexpressed.

Not everyone needs to move as they approach old age. But as eyesight begins to fade, aches set in, children move away, a fall results in a broken hip, or a spouse dies, the elderly person begins to realize that a house may be too much to handle. Seniors may feel isolated and get depressed. Many adult children, faced with the prospect of moving their parents, feel at a loss.

If you are an adult child of an aging parent whose living conditions are worrisome, this book is for you. It is to help you make the journey, familiarize you with some key issues, and provide an understanding ear when you are uncertain or feeling overwhelmed. When it came to writing about assisting elders to relocate, we knew it was important not just to tell how to do it, but to *show* how it's done right; a story was the answer. The first part of the book is an intergenerational fable of these times; it shows what happens in a typical family, the Alversons, when aging parents lose control and are no longer able to manage in the old homestead, and the adult children intervene. A central figure in the story (a sort of Yoda of moving, if you will) is the senior move manager, Moving Mentor, who is able to guide the family through the process of making the move.

This tale of the Alverson family provides needed background for approaching the roll-up-your-sleeves tasks listed in the second part of the book. Of course, if you want to sample the what-to-do-and-when-to-do-it part of the manual, you can turn to page 113 now. (If you need to get started on your project right away, you may even be tempted to skip the fable and get right to the seven-stage checklist.) For most readers, though, we don't recommend this. The story highlights so many of the typical issues and events that arise when adult children who came of age during relatively peaceful and plentiful times are confronted with moving their parents who came of age during the Depression; it illustrates so many of the feelings and reactions of the players in the drama; and it provides so many of the lessons and principles that help ease the journey, we wouldn't want you to miss it.

Table of Contents

CHAPTER ONE

Early Tremors

Sometimes change happens in people's lives like a silent slow-motion earthquake. There are tremors, but no one pays attention. They go about their business, never dreaming that the psychic landscape they are walking on will soon be shaken and the walls of expectations they've built will come tumbling down.

Such a group were the Alverson family, reunited on the day of a big wedding. There they all were, smiling and hugging and wiping their eyes as twenty-five-year-old Van Alverson and his bride Josephine tied the knot. All seemed to go well, but after the ceremony came one of those early-warning tremors we talked about. Nine-year-old Toby Ingram said to his grandmother, "I saw Grampop get dizzy coming out of the church." Lucille Alverson pretended not to hear him, but he put his little face near hers. "He almost fell down the steps," the child said, wide-eyed. "Is he *all right*?"

Lucille could not ignore this persistence, but she brushed it off. "Never mind about that now, honey. Grampop is fine. Come on and let's get you another piece of that cake!"

Later at the reception Toby's mom, Sandra Ingram, expressed her alarm to her mother, putting the same question to Lucille about her father's stumbling. She received the same sidestep her son had, but she was not to be put off. "I'm worried, Mom. Are you sure Daddy's okay?"

Lucille glanced around and lowered her voice. "Of course he's fine, dear. Don't you think I'd tell you if he wasn't? He just lost his footing for a moment. Now, let's have fun. This is a joyous occasion."

Sandy, however, kept her eye steadily on her parents. She made a note that Everett Alverson seemed disoriented at dinner. As he played host his usual joking manner lacked vitality, and once, as her father was pushing back his chair, she overheard her mother whispering, "Everett, you already *did* that toast!"

During the dancing, Sandy went looking for her mother. She found her closing the door of the suite in the hotel that had been set aside for the family, and beckoning her away. "Your dad's worn out," she said in a hushed voice. "He just needs a nap. Come on. Let's go back to the party." For the first time Sandy noticed how her mother's face beneath its makeup was etched with exhaustion. As they walked back, she felt as much concern for her mother as for her father.

They entered the bar where Marcus, the oldest son, was sparring loudly with his brother Jeff over drinks. Having already refused Marcus's traditional offer to arm-wrestle, Jeff launched his salvo subtly. "This wedding's way too traditional for me," he said with a smirk.

"Don't start with me, little brother," Marcus countered.

"I'm serious. I think it should have been held in the woods, with the bride and groom barefoot and people throwing blossoms on them while a lute player . . ." Jeff lunged aside to avoid the cuff intended as punishment for his allusion to the hippie nature of his brother's 1960's betrothal scene.

"Seriously, I'm glad you and Dad didn't fight today," Jeff said, his hand on his brother's shoulder. "Your quarrels always scared me."

Marcus sipped his drink. "No chance," he murmured. "Too much going on." He paused, then added maliciously, "Personally I was relieved, too. I didn't have to listen to you and Dad making plans for another fishing trip." Jeff frowned and fell silent, seemingly at a loss for how to respond to Marcus's oft-repeated suggestion that he, Jeff, had always been their dad's favorite. He finished his drink and wandered away.

Sandy sighed; she'd watched her brothers argue her whole life. Seeing her husband Ross on his way to freshen some drinks, she hurried over to him. ""Honey, I'm not feeling good about what's going on with Mom and Dad," she said. "Something's up, but I can't put my finger on it. I've been so busy with my business and the family that I've let things go. You know the last few times I thought I would visit my folks I never got there."

Ross frowned. "So, what are you saying?"

"I may need to look at this more closely. I want to offer to drive the folks home and spend a little time with them. I was going to take most of tomorrow off from work anyway."

Ross sighed and kissed her cheek. "That was going to be our time, but you know what you're doing."

"One son married and one to go." Marcus heaved a sigh as he sat back in the SUV's leather seats, repositioning his hands on the steering wheel. "This must be what it feels like when you're on your way to being a free man." It was the morning after the festivities, and the two brothers and their families were on the way to the airport, the women and kids visiting in the back seats. "When I retire, it'll be golf and sailing," Marcus sighed. He raised his eyes in mock prayer. "Oh Lord, let that day come soon!'"

Jeff grunted an assent and was silent, hoping they would reach the airport before the recriminations started. His hopes sank as Marcus said, "It's sure been a grind, all these years, waiting to be promoted, waiting for kids to get through college, always waiting." Jeff sank down in his seat as the other continued. "Must have been nice, having Dad take you into the business and start you off as a manager." With no response from Jeff, Marcus went on. "You know, Dad couldn't have given you that opportunity if he hadn't been building the business as I was growing up. All work and no play meant I didn't have a father who paid attention to me." They rode on in silence, until Marcus sensed he'd gone too far. When he adapted an old familiar Smothers Brothers comedy line and said, "Dad always liked you better," both men laughed, but it sounded forced.

As they neared the airport, Jeff leaned over and said, "I meant to ask you, did you notice Dad looking a little shaky today?"

Marcus frowned. "Ah, he's just getting old."

"I guess we'd know if anything was really wrong," Jeff said.

"Yeah," Marcus agreed. "Besides, if something were to happen, Sandy's always around."

———•·•———

At that moment Sandy Ingram was busily living up to her caregiver reputation. She had been surprised to find her mother giving in easily to her proposal to accompany her folks to their home in Westbrook. Now, having sent her own husband and children on the long drive home, she was steering her father's old Cadillac through familiar villages. Everett had fallen asleep in the back seat.

The two women chatted for a while, after which a long silence ensued. Sandy broke it by saying gently, "I noticed you looking tired. Are you okay, Mom?"

"I've got your Dad on my mind," said Lucille. "I'm all right, but I'm afraid you may not find the house up to snuff. It's been hard to keep up with things, I've been so busy with your father." Finally they turned into the familiar driveway. To Sandy the house she'd known as a girl looked somehow small and forlorn.

Walking in the door, she looked around critically, noting evidences of her mother's warning: dishes in the sink, summer quilt still on the bed, dusty furniture. When she asked her mother what she could do to help, Lucille waved her off, helping

Everett to bed. Sandy climbed the stairs to her old room. Standing and looking out the window at the leaves falling from the old backyard oak, she opened her cell phone and dialed her voicemail. "You have nine messages," the recorded voice announced. *No wonder it's been four months since I've been back here,* she thought. *My life is a marathon.*

After a long review of her calls, Sandy heard her mom bustling in the kitchen and knew she was done helping her father get settled for the night in the downstairs bedroom. She went downstairs, sat down and watched her mother prepare tea. "Hope you don't mind store-bought cookies," Lucille said apologetically. "You always liked my peanut-butter squares."

Sandy decided to cut to the chase. "What's going on with Dad, really?" she ventured.

Her mother sat down heavily into her chair. Her wan smile suggested that the facade would continue; then Lucille put her forehead in her hands. "Your dad's not himself these days, Sandy," she murmured. "We've been to several doctors but they haven't found anything clear-cut that's wrong. Worrying about him and caring for him is taking it out of me. I just can't manage the house any more."

Sandy looked around the place with new eyes. "Why don't you get some household help?"

"We've tried, but it's hard to find someone reliable."

"Well, how about moving?"

Lucille sighed and shook her head resignedly. "I've tried to bring it up, but your father won't hear of it. He thinks of this place as his castle, and all the while we're living in three downstairs rooms."

Lucille changed the subject by asking about her daughter's children. The two soon said good night and Sandy made her way upstairs, her thoughts in a jumble.

How had this happened so quickly? How many months had her folks been putting up a show? They had always been so healthy, so independent; it was devastating to realize they were old and needy now. Her mother wasn't coping. Her father needed care. What was she to do? She had always been the one to help out, but she had a family of her own to take care of, a fledgling fashion business to run. How could she spare the time? In disbelief she sat down on the top step and stared into the darkness. All Sandy's life her mother had been a rock, completely dependable. Now for her mom things were spinning out of control, and the feeling was contagious.

———•—•—•———

CHAPTER TWO

Seven on the Richter Scale

Back home the usual whirlwind resumed; business as usual, or in baby-boomer terms, *busy as usual.* Clients to see, meetings to attend, kids to ferry back and forth to sports practices and music lessons. Voice mail, e-mail, snail mail. Sandy and Ross barely saw each other for a week.

One day Sandy was on her way to work, her thoughts on her mother's situation. She and Lucille had talked several times, but always on the fly. As with so many well-intended items on her to-do list, Sandy's follow-up plans had been moved from one day to the next in her planner. Her cell phone interrupted her thoughts; the screen showed the caller was her mother.

Lucille's voice quavered as she said, "Your dad's had a fall. I'm calling you from the hospital. They're doing tests. I haven't heard yet from the doctor."

As Sandy hung up she thought, *What to do? Mom shouldn't be alone while Dad's in the hospital.* Hastily she made calls, putting her affairs on hold. She stopped at home briefly, then headed for Westbrook.

"Tee it up there, Jim. Let's see you sock one out there." Marcus Alverson's hearty comment was directed at his client on the golf course. As they headed down the fairway, his cell phone rang. It was Sandy with the news about their father's fall.

"I'm sorry," Marcus said, "but I can't talk now. I'll call you back."

"I was just wondering if you could provide some sort of backup for me," Sandy said.

"This is the very worst time this could have happened. My hands are tied," Marcus replied, and soon hung up. *Yeah,* he said to himself as he thought of his father, *where was my backup when I needed it from him?*

At the other end of the line, Sandy drove on, thinking, *So much for that brother.* When she reached the hospital, she did her best to allay her mother's fears. She talked with the doctor, who said, "We're going to hold your father for observation. Provided test results are negative, he'll be transferred to a rehab center for some physical therapy. The social worker says this will work out better than sending him straight home."

Thinking about her mother being alone the next few days, Sandy considered: It was a Thursday; the weekend was coming anyway. She would make arrangements to stay with her mom.

That evening at the house she heard her mother's breath coming with difficulty. "How long since you've seen a doctor, Mom—I mean for yourself?"

The next morning despite Lucille's protests, Sandy took her to see the family physician. "Yes, your mother is having shortness of breath," the doctor said, peering over his glasses. "She's exhausted. It may just be from taking care of your dad, but we'd better run some tests."

That evening Sandy phoned Jeff in Cincinnati, knowing her younger brother would be more sympathetic than Marcus. Jeff listened long and hard until she concluded, "Things are really up in the air with both Mom and Dad. It all seems so sudden. It makes me think, what would it be like if one of them were left alone?"

"Let me bounce something off you," Jeff said. "You know I've been doing Dad's taxes these past two years. Real estate prices are holding steady. If Dad turns out to be okay, what's happening may be a blessing in disguise, an opportunity to get them out of that house." The two talked about it; then Jeff said, "I'm willing to help with some money for fixing up the old place, but you'll have to figure out how to approach the subject of moving with them." When he heard Sandy's sigh, he added good-naturedly, "Lots of luck, Big Sister, bringing this up with Dad!"

⸻

"Damned contraption!" Everett Alverson shouted as the wheel of his walker caught on the slate stones of the front walk. He was home after several days in rehab, and Sandy could sense the challenges that lay ahead. While her mother got him settled in his lounge chair, Everett complained, "I'm all right! I don't need fussing over!"

Sandy spent the evening staring at the TV until her father fell asleep in his chair. The next morning a physical therapist showed up and worked with Everett. As he was leaving, another car appeared. It was the social worker, a take-charge lady who sized up the situation and told Everett, "For you to remain living here it will be necessary to modify the place. We'll send a specialist over to evaluate."

Sandy thought she saw her chance. At dinner she said, "Dad, I've been thinking. You could spend a bunch of money to change this place around . . . *or* . . . you and Mom might save yourself some headaches and have a better quality of life if you moved to a different place."

Everett's fork clattered onto his plate. "Don't you dare talk to me about moving!" he fumed. "I've lived here for forty-seven years. Why would I move now? Why start all over again when I have the security of a paid-up mortgage?"

"Okay, okay, Dad, I was just thinking," Sandy said, backing down.

"I came home from the war with nothing," her father persisted. "Your mother and I scrimped and saved to buy this place." Looking at Lucille he added, "This house has all our memories. Are you asking us to leave the place where we brought you and your brothers home to live when you were babies, where we raised you and watched you grow? Hah? It's out of the question!"

CHAPTER THREE

What You Resist, Persists

The silent earthquake had struck. Over a life accustomed to steady creative energy and productivity now brooded a heaviness and confusion. Where had Sandy been these last few years that she assumed that things would continue to fall neatly into place? Something had been growing right in front of her face and she had not been aware of it. She, who had proven herself a capable manager of both her family and her own business, was unable to manage this situation with her own parents.

That morning Sandy received a phone call from her friend Diane. She was surprised to find herself getting an earful from another trouble spot; it seemed like more than mere coincidence. "Harry and I have made an agonizing decision," Diane told her. "We're cutting into Brenda's college fund to build an addition onto the house for Harry's mom." As her friend recounted the unfolding saga that led to the conclusion that her mother-in-law was to come and live with them, it was Sandy's turn to comfort and commiserate. When she hung up, she wondered. *Will that happen to Ross and me?*

> # Maplewood Village
> *A Senior Retirement Community*

The sign caught Sandy's eye as she drove from a meeting with a supplier. On impulse she pulled into the circular driveway and parked. A modern low building was framed by tall cedars and pleasant gardens. Walking into the lobby she was greeted by the receptionist. "What can we do for you?"

"I'm not sure," Sandy answered truthfully. "My parents are still in their own home and not faring well there. I've had the thought that moving might be a good plan for them, but I just don't know."

The woman nodded sympathetically. "Our marketing director's not available this afternoon, but I'd be happy to make an appointment for you. Meanwhile, you're welcome to look over the literature there on the table."

"Thanks." Sandy strolled over and thumbed through a series of brochures and pamphlets.

She was about to walk away when a small informal-looking booklet caught her eye. *Moving . . . Ready or Not?* it asked. She began reading it on the way out the door and suddenly stopped. For the first time in days she found herself smiling.

Reaching the parking lot, Sandy continued reading, chuckling at the pictures. The first part of the little book described reasons seniors give for why they're not ready to move.

I'M NOT READY...

because nothing's really changed. I feel I'm the same person I've always been.

I'M NOT READY...

because I have all the things around me here that please me.

I'M NOT READY...

because I'm too busy living my life to start going through all my stuff.

I'M NOT READY...

because the kids still come for the holidays with their kids. My home is the re-union site.

I'M NOT READY...

because I have plenty of friends. We jump in the car to visit each other all the time.

I'M NOT READY...

because I own my house free and clear. Why would I take on more expense?

I'M NOT READY...

because going to a place like *that* means that my life is over.

I'M NOT READY...

because my kids won't take my things, and I can't bear to see them go to strangers.

I'M NOT READY...

because if I let go of this place I'll be giving up all my cherished memories.

I'M NOT READY...

because I don't need more change in my life---I need less.

I'M NOT READY...

because my kids would fight over where I should go. If I stay here, it's settled.

I'M NOT READY...

because I don't have the energy or help to face moving. I wouldn't even know where to start.

"Wow!" Sandy thought. There are arguments here that Dad hasn't even thought of yet!

As she pulled into the driveway at home she heard a shout, and her fourteen-year-old daughter Ashley dashed out the front door. "Where've you been, Mom? I'm late again to warm-up!" she complained, hopping in on the passenger side.

"Oh, honey, I'm sorry," Sandy apologized, backing the car out again.

"What is with you these days anyway?" the teen complained. "You're always on the phone with Nana. You don't listen to us any more. I swear you act like you're out of it half the time."

———•—•———

That evening at the close of the meal her husband Ross told Sandy, "We need to talk." As they took cups of coffee into the family room and sat down, Sandy wondered if she were in for a reprimand. Feeling overwhelmed the previous evening, she had canceled a dinner date with their favorite couple, hoping to get caught up with some of the things left undone because of her parents' crisis. Now she found Ross sitting close beside her and patting her shoulder. "I know you've been feeling down because of all that's been happening with your folks" he said. "I can't fix things for you, but I found something at work that may be helpful to you."

Sandy felt her hopes rise. "Is it one of those employee assistance programs?" she asked.

"No. It's something my boss talks about—a problem-solving skill called **REFRAMING**. Look at this." He handed her a picture.

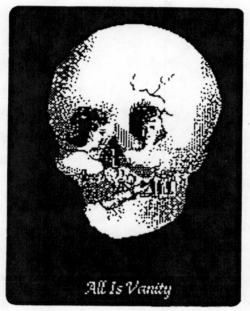

All Is Vanity

"What do you see?" Ross asked.

"I see a skull."

"Good. Now, look again."

Suddenly Sandy exclaimed, "Oh, it's a lady looking in a mirror!"

Ross smiled. "You just did it," he said. "You *reframed* the picture. That means you shifted the way you saw it, without changing the facts of it."

"I certainly prefer the woman-and-mirror way of looking at it," Sandy said.

"That's the real power of reframing," said Ross. "When you reframe something you change the meaning of it for you. Consequently, your attitude toward it changes."

"I see," Sandy said, "That's pretty neat."

"Now," Ross continued. "Let's see if we can apply the skill of reframing to this whole scenario with your parents. Let's look at the sequence of events of the past two months. First, the wedding brings you and your parents together so you can see the changes that are happening in them. Who knows how much longer it would have been before you got home to see them? Next your dad falls, but now he's out of the woods. The doctors say whatever is going on with your mom isn't serious. Finally, we find out Diane and Harry are going through something similar. At least you don't have to feel so alone. When you first heard about each of these things, there seemed to be no way to look at it but the downside."

"The skull."

"Right. But maybe you can reframe what's happening and see something like the lady. What do you think?"

Sandy sat up. "You might be right. Look what I happened upon today." She handed him the little booklet, *Moving, Ready or Not?* Soon they were laughing together at the pictures. By the time they'd finished the second half of the book, Sandy had some new things to say to her father.

On the other hand, you <u>might</u> be saying . . .

I'M SO GLAD I ACTED IN TIME!

I'M SO GLAD I ACTED IN TIME... because at least my kids didn't put all my things in a dumpster, like my friend's kids did.

I'M SO GLAD I ACTED IN TIME... because I'm no longer comfortable driving, and I would have been lonely not visiting my friends.

I'M SO GLAD I ACTED IN TIME... because it turns out once I let go of my stuff, I didn't miss it at all.

I'M SO GLAD I ACTED IN TIME... because I lost my spouse six months after the move. I'd have had to do it all myself.

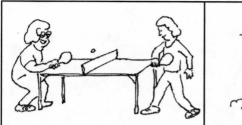

I'M SO GLAD I ACTED IN TIME...

because this place isn't like I thought. I'm treated with respect---never as if I'm old.

I'M SO GLAD I ACTED IN TIME...

because I'm not a burden to my kids. They're so happy to see me settled in so well.

I'M SO GLAD I ACTED IN TIME...

because it's such a relief to have this small world, where all my needs are met.

I'M SO GLAD I ACTED IN TIME...

because the next winter we had so much snow I couldn't have made those trips to my doctor.

I'M SO GLAD I ACTED IN TIME...
because I wanted to take up the piano, but never could find the time. Here, I'm part of a band.

I'M SO GLAD I ACTED IN TIME...
because after I moved the water heater broke and the roof started to leak.

I'M SO GLAD I ACTED IN TIME...
because I would have been lonely. A best friend moved away. Another had a stroke.

I'M SO GLAD I ACTED IN TIME...
because I got to take charge of all decisions regarding my move.

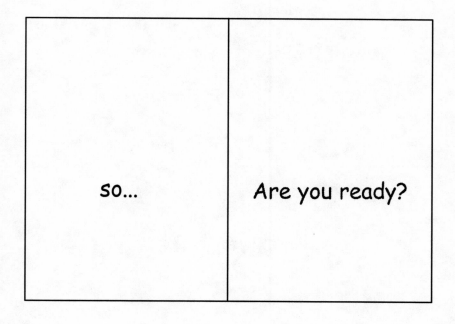

so...   Are you ready?

CHAPTER FOUR

Finger in the Dike

These visits to the doctor have made me realize my strength isn't what it used to be." Lucille Alverson was talking with her husband in their living room. She had found a moment when it seemed Everett might be more receptive to her ideas than usual. "I worry you could fall again and I might not even be here to help or make a call."

"Honey," he said slyly, "I didn't tell you, but I faked that last fall. I just like the ride in the ambulance with the siren going."

"Everett, I am *serious*!"

"Oh, Lucy, calm yourself," Everett consoled. "I'm through fallin'. Don't you see me gettin' around better with this walker?"

"It's not only that, Ev," Lucy persisted. "I look around this house and I'm embarrassed at how it looks. Things are being let go. I can't keep up with it."

"Maybe we need to hire somebody in to help."

Lucille balked at this. "It's an idea, but I'd sure feel funny about a stranger coming in here with things in such a state."

The phone rang, and Lucille reached for it. It was her friend Margie Gilbert, inviting her to play bridge the next day.

"That'd be nice," Lucille said. "I'd love to come."

Margie said, "Don't forget, I've got a new address. I can't wait for you to see my new place."

Lucille hung up and told Everett about her invitation. She thought, *Margie had some help before she moved. Maybe I can talk with her about getting that person.*

She glanced over at Everett and gasped. He was standing in the middle of the floor, bent over, with his hands hanging down near his shoes. "What in the world are you doing?" she said.

"I made what I consider a great effort to get down here to tie my shoe," he said. "Then when I got here I started wondering what else I could do while I was down here."

Lucille shook her head at her husband's quirky attempts at humor, which included making fun of his own aging process. She recalled seeing an ad on TV for an electronic alarm to be worn and used in case of emergency. She made a mental note to ask how to get one for Everett.

———•—•———

Sandy looked at her bedside clock. It said 2:30 am. She rose quietly so as not to bother Ross and went to the kitchen for a snack. On the table she saw the booklet she'd brought home from Maplewood Village. It reminded her of the interaction she and her husband had had earlier. *That reframing business is interesting*, she told herself. *I am lucky to have Ross as my friend and partner. He's being so good through all this time.* She thumbed through the little book again, then in the back page she found a website address of its publisher.

Moving to the kitchen laptop computer she went to the site. Its logo was a house sheltering a group of elders. Her eyes opened wide when she read the headline: *Helping Seniors to Move With Ease*. As she scrolled down through the homepage, certain items caught her attention. One was headed, "Thinking about moving? Remember . . . "

o   Change is happening, even if you do nothing.

o   Start downsizing yesterday.

o   Most of your things are worth less than you think.

o   Your kids will mostly NOT want, or need, or have room for, the things you wish they will take.

o   If you don't take charge of things now, a lot of your possessions might end up in a dumpster.

Further on, Sandy found an item titled "Five different stategies for moving seniors."

1.   Everything moves out of the house at the same time.

2.   Client moves to new home first, old home is sold later.

3.   Kitchen and bathroom move first, client moves several days later.

4.   Move takes two days, so client has a place to rest in each location.

5.   Half of household moves, and half stays intact, to build a bridge between new place and old.

"Why," Sandy thought with surprise, "look at all these choices." Feeling the doors of her imagination opening, she read on, noting a list of statistics:

78 million Baby Boomers.
One turns 50 every seven seconds.
70% of people over 75 still own their own home.

Sandy found herself connecting these numbers with her own small world. Not only her own parents' dilemma, but her friend Diane's situation. Then other pieces began to fit. There was Jill, the bookkeeper she'd just hired, whose coming to work had been delayed a few days because of having to unravel her parents' finances. There was even that man she'd sat next to at Ross's company dinner talking about how many dumpsters he'd needed to get his parents relocated.

For the next thirty minutes as she toured the website, Sandy Ingram found it hard to believe that someone actually had a business dedicated to helping people facing in situations so similar to her own. The author, Moving Mentor, seemed to be speaking directly to her. One item she found absorbing was a short article under *Thoughts for the Day* entitled "Seniors' Home—Castle or Prison?"

> For a householder from the so-called Greatest Generation, staying in the familiar domain where he has long been master seems to ensure his privacy and independence. It may be just the opposite.
>
> Suppose you place a toddler in a backyard fenced area to ensure his safe and independent movement. For the same child in later teen years such a fence would make him not independent but more dependent. So it can be with the senior.

Often, although the older couple speaks of the house as their safe haven, it may actually have become a prison. Stairways may offer a challenge. If they've gotten behind on the maintenance of the house, the place that once was their pride and joy is now a source of embarrassment. The handymen who helped them and whom they trusted have died, retired, or moved on.

So, ironically, although a senior may vigorously oppose the idea, a move to a different and more appropriate locale could help maintain his/her independence, or even increase it.

Sandy was excited. She turned back to the home page and clicked on the *Contact Us* button. She typed an e-mail:

Dear Moving Mentor:

On a recent visit to my aging parents' home I found their situation rapidly deteriorating. I don't see how they can stay in the home, but I can't even raise the subject without my Dad blowing up. With my own family to care for and a business to run, I can't be dashing back and forth between my life and theirs . . . Help!

Sandy Ingram

———•◦•———

Lucille was visiting her friend Margie. Walking into the Mumford Hills Senior Community's main building, she found herself admiring the tastefully furnished lobby. *Everything looks so taken care of,* she thought. A smiling receptionist directed her to the game room where a group of women were preparing for their bridge game. Lucille saw her friend beckoning at her from across the room. Soon Margie was introducing her around to her friends, some of whom she already knew.

Drawing her friend aside, Lucille told her, "You look so relaxed! Has it really been only ten days since you moved? I would have thought you'd still be recovering."

Margie laughed. "I can hardly believe it myself. They told me I'd be settled in a few days but I really didn't believe it."

"They?" Lucille inquired. Who's 'they?'"

"The consultant and her staff who planned and organized my move from start to finish. She calls herself Moving Mentor." She handed Lucille a letter. "She wrote me the nicest note."

Dear Margie,

Well, you're finally settled into your new digs. I have an image from the past, of you sitting at your kitchen table in your old place, looking so forlorn, wondering to me why your husband had to die a year ago and leave you alone and helpless.

If you'd stayed in that house, things would have continued to deteriorate, but the thought of moving—away from your memories, away from the choices your husband and you had made for more than fifty years—was breaking your heart. Either way, things were out of control.

When I said goodbye to you yesterday, a week after your move, you were in wonderment. We had been able to capture, in a new location, the essence of what you and Herb had built, and to infuse it with new life. Congratulations, Margie. You've succeeded in transmitting important pieces of your own life to your children and grandchildren, and many without means will benefit from the donations you have made.

Warmest regards, and many happy times ahead!

Moving Mentor

After the card game was over and the other women had left, Margie Gilbert invited her guest to see her new apartment. Lucille was immediately struck by the gracious, calm atmosphere of the cozy place. Plainly there had been much forethought expended here. Everything had its place. Somehow her friend's apartment truly was a re-creation of the elegance and grace of Margie's original home. The simplicity and functionality of the place contrasted strongly with her own sense of being overwhelmed at home by so much clutter. As they enjoyed tea and cake, Lucille admired the cup and saucer's elegant design. "Isn't this your good china?" she said.

Margie smiled. "I was encouraged during the move to take these things out and just enjoy them." This was a radical idea for her fellow Depression-era friend Lucille. Later as Lucille was driving home from her visit, she thought sadly of the clutter at home. She realized something with a start: *Having less stuff can actually make life better.* She resolved to share this with Everett.

───── ·•· ─────

It was Saturday, and football season. The big game between the Westbrook Wildcats and the Lexington Blaze was in the third quarter. Sandy and Ross cheered as Toby, their nine-year-old, took the field with his team. Sandy was proud of the look of the new uniforms; her sports fashion boutique had contributed the design.

Ross spotted his friend Jim LeCourt a few seats away in the stands, and waved hello. "Wonder how Jim and Arlene are doing since he lost his father," Ross whispered. During a change of players, they moved over to talk with the couple. "That was a great pass your Danny made," Sandy said.

"Yeah," said Jim. "He's doing pretty well, considering he and I haven't had our usual passing practice time this year. I've been really tied up with my mom."

Ross said, "We were wondering how things are going since you lost your dad."

Arlene LeCourt sighed. "You know how that generation is. Jim's dad handled all the house maintenance and the checkbook. Now he's gone and Mom is helpless." She looked at her husband tenderly. "This good man and his siblings have been working to keep things afloat."

"My sister, brother and I are alternating weekends now," Jim said. "My folks kept talking about downsizing and moving to a smaller place, but they waited too long. They wouldn't even listen to us when we suggested they stay put and get help in as they needed it. Now my mom's in this mess. If only we'd pushed them to make some changes, we wouldn't all be so pressured now."

As the referee's whistle shrilled, Ross and Sandy exchanged glances.

———•·•·•———

Driving home from a series of errands, Sandy thought about the past week's phone conversations she'd had with her brothers about their parents' plight. She reviewed the list of ideas they had come up with for making things easier: Online banking. Meals on wheels. Housekeeping help. Home health aides. Scheduling friends and neighbors to help with shopping. Sandy had felt so good after brainstorming these things. It seemed at last they had a workable plan. But it hadn't taken long for her to realize that keeping track of it all just added more hours to her own weekly schedule.

Reaching home, she started to put the groceries away, meanwhile phoning her mother.

"Hi Mom. How are things today?"

"Good. Your dad and I sat on the back porch for a while and got some fresh air."

"I hope you bundled up. These days are getting chilly."

"Well, it was a little chilly in the house, too. We couldn't get the furnace started, but Dave Dryden from next door came over and was able to get it going, and it's fine now."

Furnace trouble. That's all we need now, Sandy thought. "How did Dad's visit to the doctor go?"

"Oh fine." Pause. "Well, there's this new medication we're supposed to get."

"Uh-huh. When is he supposed to take it?"

"I, uh . . . can't remember just now. Oh darn!"

"That's okay. It'll come."

"No, that's not what's bothering me!"

"What's wrong?""

"Unless I do remember it, I'll have to face calling the doctor, and I hate that!"

A long silence ensued. Sandy felt herself moving into the void created by that silence. "Don't worry, Mom," she said reassuringly. "I'll get right back to you with the information. What's the doctor's number?"

She hung up, then dialed the number of the office. A recorded voice crackled over the wire. "If this is an emergency, dial 911. If you need to make or break an appointment, dial 1. If you need billing information, dial 4. If you need a prescription renewed, dial 3. To speak to the nurse . . . "

When she finally did get through to the doctor's assistant and asked for the prescription, Sandy was told there was no permission given in the chart for the office staff to speak to anyone but the patient. "We can't release that information because of the Privacy Act."

———•◦•———

CHAPTER FIVE

Time Famine

Sandy awoke from her dream with a start. A giant wave had been breaking over her. Her feet couldn't touch bottom any more. Things that had always been securely in place were floating away from her. Voices were calling to her frantically. Her daughter had missed a music lesson. She had forgotten to clean her son's uniform for the big game, and he was in tears. Someone was trying to throw her a life preserver, but it was just out of reach . . . She sat up, drenched with sweat.

Rising, Sandy went to her laptop and reviewed a list of unopened emails. There was one from Moving Mentor. The subject line said: *Help is on the way.* She opened the letter and read:

Dear Sandy,

I hear you loud and clear. It can be discouraging to think you know what your parents need, and have them resist it.

But if you think about it from their point of view, you'll understand. Their home has been your parents' castle. All their lives it's been the symbol of stability, security and accomplishment. It's natural for them to resist any suggestion of living anywhere else.

Sandy stopped reading for a moment to listen to her mind. *Of course,* it was saying. *Hanging on to the old homestead is the most natural thing in the world. Why haven't I seen that?* She read on.

What's happening in your life and your parents' life is a process. I know this will sound strange but I'd like you, while they're resisting, to do something in your own house that can help get them going. Clean out an area, or give away three things you don't need. It may not seem related, but it is.

We at Moving Mentor can act with you and your parents as facilitators of this process. Email me your best time for a phone talk.

Warm regards,

Moving Mentor

P.S. Greenville Savings Bank is sponsoring a workshop for seniors and their families called "Yes, You Can Think About Moving." I'm presenting as a panel member. Please come as my guest. Bring your parents if you would like. We can talk together afterwards.

Sandy got up and went to make herself a cup of tea. She felt a wondrous lightness. Not only was she not alone, she could sense the dawning of a new, more strategic way to respond. Ross's kind suggestion of the other night about "reframing" things was being reinforced. Maybe, despite the seeming jumble of disorganization, a promising path was emerging. Later, sipping the fragrant tea, she wondered, *Who is this Moving Mentor who seems to understand so much and communicate in such a way to put me at ease?*

Sandy Ingram had listened patiently to presentations by a realtor, an attorney, a financial planner and a mortgage officer from a bank. All were focused on the subject of seniors taking charge of change. When she looked around, Sandy saw that most of the crowd were around her own age. Now her attention was focused on the trim, neatly attired woman of about fifty who moved to the podium.

She smiled as she introduced herself. "I have a name, but everybody calls me Moving Mentor. What we've been hearing from my fellow panelists has all been focused on the assumption that a senior is thinking about moving. But I have little doubt that many of you who are adult children have found that you can't even bring up the subject with your parents. I'm sure that many of your folks are saying, 'I'm never moving from this place. They're going to carry me out of here feet first.'"

As Sandy joined in the group chuckle, she marveled at the realization: *I'm not the only one!*

Moving Mentor went on, "Actually, this statement, 'I'm never moving,' can be a first step of the process of moving on. If you were to think of it that way, a host of things would become apparent to you that you can accomplish now, while things seem to be static. The first thing to do is give yourself permission to decide not to decide about any particular plan." Moving Mentor explained that adult children can use this time period of seeming indecision to do some important tasks, such as getting paperwork in order.

"Talk with your parents about having a will, a health-care proxy, and choosing a power of attorney. Because of the Privacy Act, help them get authorization in doctors' files for communication to take place between physicians and close family members."

After a brief question-and-answer period, the program ended. People crowded around Moving Mentor for a while, asking questions. When she was free, Sandy introduced herself; they shook hands and went across the street to a coffee shop. When they were seated in a booth and had ordered, Sandy looked admiringly at Moving Mentor.

"How did you get started in this business?" she wanted to know.

"I was one of those adult children I help now in my work. My father had passed away, and my mother needed to move. She'd been in the same house for forty years. I had been dreading that time coming, but what I thought would be a painful and exhausting chore turned into a wonderful experience. We laughed and we cried, and it was a real opportunity to share and renew our relationship. When it was over I thought, *I could do this for others.* It wasn't long before I found myself in business."

"How do you describe your service?"

"We help seniors and their families through every step of the moving process, from making the decision to move, to deciding what to keep, and what will happen to the stuff they're not keeping, to floor planning, to packing, and helping people get settled in their new place. Sometimes we help folks downsize and stay where they are. Consulting with adult children is an important part of the process. Enough about me, though. Tell me more about your parents' situation."

Sandy spent the next twenty minutes recounting the details of her own dilemma, including her own life and that of her siblings, a description of her parents' home, and what she had found during her visits there. "I'm just in the dark as to what to do next," she added.

Moving Mentor had been listening carefully. Now she said, "You heard me say there's a stage of this process that's called *'I'm never moving.'* Sandy smiled, recalling the "feet-first" comment. "We don't know right now what is the best path for your parents to take. That will become clear as we proceed."

Sandy found the vagueness of this statement disquieting. It left her without what she called an *edc* – an estimated date of completion. In true Baby Boomer fashion, she wanted to be able to complete a list of tasks, see the light at the end of the tunnel, and get back to her life as usual.

As if reading Sandy's mind, Moving Mentor reached into her case and handed Sandy a paper. "Here's a to-do list I prepared with you in mind. Whether your parents move or stay put, these are things you can do now."

Sandy scanned the list hurriedly.

- Contact a local senior center where they live and find out about services offered – meals on wheels, etc.
- Visit local retirement communities in their area and educate yourself about costs, length of time of waiting lists, friends who might be there, etc.
- Contact their clergyperson and ask about what is happening for seniors in the area's houses of worship.

Are most seniors staying in the community or leaving to go south or to be near family members?

- Have a conversation with your brothers to bring them up to date – maybe email them first so they can digest information and then set up a conference call between the three of you to discuss the situation.

- Make a list of immediate needs your parents have (meals, cleaning services, help with shower, etc). Get your parents' input on these. Brainstorm with your brothers how these jobs might get filled – who might do what and when (after you find out what your parents might be able to do for themselves with the help of the senior center resource list).

- On your next visit (or maybe assign this to one of your siblings), ask your parents if you can help them put their paperwork in order. Most important paperwork – health care proxy, power of attorney, will, tax papers, spread sheet with bank account numbers, pins, passwords and other important information, authorization to talk to doctors.

- Talk to a local realtor to see if he/she would be willing to provide you with information about what houses comparable to your parents' are selling for, so you can get some idea of what their house might be worth.

"I can handle this," Sandy said.

"Not the whole list." Moving Mentor raised three fingers. "Just three items."

"That's all?"

Moving Mentor smiled. "Have you ever heard the expression, 'How do you eat an elephant?'"

"Sure," Sandy said. "One bite at a time. "

"That's the principle I call **NIBBLE**. It means to take a little bite, doing just what is needed at the time. People nowadays are constantly wolfing their tasks, because they're always feeling they never can do enough. Instead of paying attention to what's in front of them, their minds are always on *what's next*. However, paying attention to what's in front of you is what is critical in this process.

"Whether they move or not, your parents are in a time of great transition. Much of this transition is psychological, not just physical. You are like a midwife. You can't rush the birth of the life they are moving into. I am limiting you to three tasks so you can pay proper attention to those, and balance them with whatever else is going on in the rest of your own life. Later on you'll be applying this nibbling process to your parents, getting them to do just one or two things at a time, to contribute to their transition."

That night as she was dropping off to sleep, Sandy found she was calmer, yet energized. She had a focus now that had been missing. She had some things to do, and they were doable.

Moving Mentor's Journal

Sandy and her siblings have an opportunity many adult children will not be fortunate enough to have. I'm thinking of the brothers I saw last week; one of their parents gone, the other hastily moved to a nursing home. No one to talk to but each other, only the two of them left to sort out a lifetime of stuff in an overcrowded house. It would have been so great if they all could have anticipated what was coming and created a convenient timetable for working in their parents' interest.

The Alversons still have a chance to make a difference. I want to shout it to people even younger than Sandy and her brothers: I'm glad you are getting going! So many of your peers can't be convinced to break away from their busy routines. They don't realize that whatever they do for their parents at this stage creates a readiness for them to move on in their lives as well. I know what so many would say to me: "My parents refuse to talk about this with us, and I am too busy, and my house is too full to take any of their stuff. It's just a no-win situation." And I know what I would tell them . . . but no time now. Maybe I'll add it as an article to my website.

CHAPTER SIX

Light in the Tunnel?

The doorbell rang. Everett glanced out the window. "Oh fine. It's that Meals on Wheels guy again!" On the way to answer the knock, struggling with his walker, he muttered, "I'm coming. I'm coming. It's not the way I used to, but I'm coming."

After the delivery man left, Lucille opened the lunch packages. Everett sniffed at it, sampled a few bites of it, and pushed it away in disgust. Watching him, she said, "It's not the meal."

"Huh?"

"Remember what the preacher, Brother Samuel, told us when we got married?"

"No."

"He said that when we start being irritated by the small stuff, there's something else going on. When I see you setting aside this delicious home-cooked meal, I think you can't eat because something is eating *you*."

"What do you mean?" Everett said belligerently.

Lucille took a breath and went on. "We're having to swallow our pride, aren't we? The house is going down, and our bodies are, as well. I didn't realize how much our lives had changed until I walked into Margie Gilbert's apartment."

Everett snorted and struggled to his feet. He grabbed his walker. "I'm going for my nap," he said.

Lucille watched him shuffle off and bang the bedroom door shut. *Did I push things too far?* she mused. Maybe so, but she was glad to have that off her chest. She hated having tension with Everett. She wished she could talk to her daughter about it, but she held back, not wanting to burden Sandy. Instead she reached for the phone and dialed Marcus. Maybe her oldest boy could talk to his father.

After several tries, she reached him on his car phone. "Hello dear," she said. "Just thinking of you today, wondering how you're doing."

Marcus groaned. "Surviving, Ma, just surviving. I'm always running to catch up. 'Course I did manage to get away for the weekend for a little fishing. You know, Mom, all work and no play!" There was a pause. "Listen, it's great that Dad's out of the hospital. You know what? You guys should take in a movie. I saw a good one the other day . . . "

While Marcus rambled on in his self-absorbed way, Lucille told herself he was too out of touch to be of help, and gave it up.

Later, sitting and listening to her husband's gentle snoring from the next room, she thought suddenly of a gift Brother Samuel had given them years ago. She went to the bookshelf where it had been collecting dust, brought it into the kitchen and cleaned it off. It was a plaque that said . . .

Commitment

Until one is committed, there is the chance to draw back, always hesitation. Concerning all acts of initiative and creation there is one elementary truth, the ignorance of which kills countless ideas and splendid plans:

The moment one commits, then

Providence acts, too.

All sorts of things occur to help one that would never otherwise have occurred. A whole stream of events issues from the decision, raising in one's favor all manner of unforeseen incidents and meetings and material assistance which no man could have dreamed would have come his way.

Whatever you can do, or dream you can, begin it. Boldness has genius, power and magic in it. Begin it now.

--- Johann Goethe

Lucille's mind went back to another time when she and Everett were at a crisis point. They were low on money, and she proposed that she look for a job. Everett was adamant in his refusal. She went ahead anyway, and wound up being proud of herself for making a substantial contribution to the family. Everett had changed his tune that time! She recalled his beaming face, his boasting about her to their friends.

She told herself. *I'm going to have to act here, with or without Everett's permission, just like I did before. And when this is all over, I'll see that same sweet smile on his face.*

Lucille reached up, removed a wall-hanging from one of their travels from its place above the stove, and hung the plaque in its place. For the first time in a long time, she felt empowered. She felt true **ESTEEM**.

———•—•———

By email in succeeding weeks, Moving Mentor continued to assign tasks to her new client Sandy, two or three at a time. One of her suggestions resulted in a strategic visit of Sandy's family to the senior Alversons. They brought lunch and had a memorable time. The children asked questions of their grandparents they'd found in a book Sandy had brought called *Memoirs of Home*. This got Everett telling stories about when their mom was a little girl. His reminiscing about old times in the house provided the opportunity for Ross and the kids to use their new digital camera to take pictures of each room. The idea was to surprise their grandfather with an album celebrating the homestead of which he was so proud.

During another sleepless night, Sandy rose and went to her computer. She dialed Moving Mentor's website, and looked over the homepage offerings. A tab called "Intergenerational Issues" caught her eye and she clicked on it.

She read: *G.I Generation Meets the Baby Boomer Generation*—"Conflict or Cooperation?" A table appeared below the provocative title, and she found herself scanning it thoughtfully.

The G.I. Generation	The Baby Boomers
• Stalwartly independent, self-reliant	• Interdependent, hire services
• Private, usually keep things to themselves	• Open, talk about feelings
• Savers, grew up in the Depression	• Spenders - buy now, pay later
• Self-sacrificing	• Self-gratifying and self-care
• Have saved for "old age"	• Worried about retirement
• Community minded, church goers	• Virtual community, global outlook
• Their home is their castle	• Have moved around, change is usual
• Patriotic, fought in WWII	• More anti-authority, raised in the 60s
• Their word and a firm handshake sealed the connection	• Legal minded, loyalty uncertain
• Slower pace of life	• On the go from babyhood

Wow, Sandy thought, *"conflict or cooperation" is the right question!* Below the lists she found the heading "Reader Comments."

We at Moving Mentor receive many emails from adult children referring to the inter-generational issues involved in relocating their parents. The following letters are typical of the variety of viewpoints among writers.

1.   Dear Moving Mentor:

I appreciate so much the help you provided in getting my dad settled in his new condo. Growing up in our household was a stormy time for my brother and me. My father had been a soldier, and when we reached college age and protested the war our own house became the scene of many battles. Since then we've gone our separate ways, hardly speaking. When my mother died, my brother would not hear of helping. I learned of your service through a friend, and you helped my dad move. You suggested that I come twice, for a day each time, to help. For me, it was the right balance; I gave my dad a little extra, and was able to maintain my own footing. Thank you.

2.   Dear Moving Mentor:

There has perhaps never been so pronounced a clash between the values and perspectives of two succeeding generations, as this between the Baby Boomers and their Depression-era parents. Protest and rebellion always to some extent characterize the coming-of-age set, but my generation was the first to raise it to the level of a national emergency! How much more poignant, then, is the opportunity now for us, who profess to value self-responsibility and personal growth, to achieve understanding and empathy—yes, and healing—by acting consciously and purposefully in behalf of our parents when such an important transition is on the horizon as their moving at this age. In the past, whatever life-passages they went through, they went through without us, but this important one we can make together. Your *work must bring countless families together. I know it has mine. Thank you and God bless you.*

———·•·———

One day during one of Everett and Lucille's visits to the doctor's office, they had a surprise. A young man sitting in the waiting room spoke up. "Aren't you Mr. Alverson?"

"That's me," Everett said.

"I remember you talking with my dad, Anthony Crosby. I'm Richard, his son."

Everett was delighted. "So you're Tony Crosby's boy. How is my old pal?"

"He's moved down south to be near my brother in Florida."

"What's your line of work, Richard?" Lucille asked.

"I'm in real estate. Working with my dad in his retirement and resettling got me interested in working with seniors. I've just finished taking a class and have become certified as a Senior Residential Specialist in Real Estate."

"Does that mean old houses and old people go together?" Everett joked.

Richard smiled. "Working with seniors who have been in their homes for a long time is a special privilege and it requires special skills."

"Maybe you could help us," Lucille spoke up. Ignoring Everett's frown, she invited Richard Crosby to visit their home and give them some advice.

On the way home, Everett said, "Imagine bumping into Tony's kid. He must be proud. But don't be getting any ideas about selling our home."

After a while Everett spoke again. "Remember, Lucy, how we struggled to pay for our house, thinking it was so much money? We could be sitting on a gold mine now!"

Lucille Alverson drove on in silence, but her lips were drawn into a smile.

> *Moving Mentor's Journal*
>
> *Again and again I encounter families who have waited so long that, instead of choosing to move, they are forced into it. My 78-year-old client Freidrich is a one person who knows the value of taking charge of change, rather than falling victim to circumstances beyond his control. During our packing for his move, he invited us to have tea with him. I commented on the unusual tableware he brought out. "It's from Austria," he said, "where I grew up." Then his story poured out. When he was five, world events resulted in his father's moving to America, and Frieidrich and his mother were forced to follow. It took them a long time, and constant moves, to finally settle in this country—only to have his father die, forcing Frieidrich and his mother once again to downsize and relocate. "This time," he admitted tearfully, "is the first time I am moving by my own volition."*

Sandy was delighted to hear from her mother about what had transpired in the doctor's office. She relayed it to her brothers in a conference call, and they agreed that it was the best news they could have received. As she and her siblings talked together, they brainstormed about next steps.

Marcus said, "If they do decide to move, where will they go?"

Sandy told of her visit to Maplewood Village. Jeff, who had been mostly quiet, said, "I've heard that if you're looking to move into a retirement community, it can take as much as two years on the waiting list before your turn comes up."

Marcus sounded concerned. "Those places can be really expensive, you know. What makes us think Mom and Dad could afford it? They've always been so private about their finances."

Jeff said, "Don't forget, Dad agreed to have me do their taxes last year. I think they could swing it if the place were moderately priced. Anyway, there is a financial consultant where I work. Why don't I crunch some numbers with this guy, using information from a retirement community near me? I may as well get something for my family from my job. I asked for some leave time to help Mom and Dad, but they didn't go for it."

Sandy said, "My friend Diane is building an addition to her house for her husband's mom to move in with them. I've thought about Mom and Dad moving in with us, or near us, but what would their life be like away from the people and places they've known for so long?"

"Wait a minute here," Marcus interjected. "If the folks were to use the money they have for a new place, what does all this mean for our inheritance? I was hoping money from them would take pressure off me for my own retirement."

Sandy sighed. "We don't have to have all the answers now," she said patiently. "I'm talking with a consultant named Moving Mentor who's helping me figure things out for the folks. She can help us with some of these questions we have."

"Fine," Marcus said. "And where is the money coming from to pay for *that*?"

At this, Jeff jumped in, saying, "Hey, sometimes you have to spend money to get the help you need." Suddenly all three were arguing, and the conference ended on a sour note.

Upset and hurt, Sandy put in a call to Moving Mentor. She shared how she and her brothers were at odds, adding, "Everything seems to be stuck."

"You never know," Moving Mentor said. "Things look stuck, but maybe they aren't. It's good to remember that you can never see the whole picture from where you're standing. All you can do is feel the current disappointment. It reminds me of a story an elderly client told me, about something that happened when she was twenty and working for the War Office. She found a certain co-worker attractive, and one day he asked her out dancing. When her parents learned they would be at a nightclub in the city, they insisted she have a chaperone. She found another couple to accompany them to the nightclub, and her excitement grew when she found someone to cover her shift at work. But at the last minute that person cancelled, and she had to work. "I was devastated," she said. "But if I'd gone dancing that night, I wouldn't be here. You see, it was the Coconut Grove, and that was the night the place burned down and all those people died."

"Wow," Sandy said. "You're right, you just never know. I'm going to count my blessings and figure all is for the best."

"Good," said Moving Mentor. "While things look stuck, let me introduce a strategy I call Going With Your Strengths."

She coached Sandy in having each sibling assume tasks that were right for that person. While Jeff did the financials, Sandy would help her mom to do some downsizing. "Let's wait on Marcus for now," she added. "It will become clear what his role is."

When Ross came home that evening Sandy vented to him about the phone spat. "Marcus doesn't need the money," she complained. "Why is he always the one to complain about spending it?"

"Marcus, of all people, should know better than to worry about his retirement," Ross said. "He owns a lakeside cabin worth a bundle. He's forgotten about how he and Julia got that piece of property. Remember the story he told us?"

Sandy nodded, recalling the oft-told tale. "They were driving by that lake and Marcus was saying "We could never have a place here" and suddenly Julia sat up straight and said, "What do you mean? Why, I'll have you know we _own_ this lake, along with the woods, the sky, and everything else you see." And right then, while Marcus was trying to figure out how to respond to her fit of cosmic optimism, they saw the place that they ended up renting for a few summers, and finally buying."

Ross smiled. "I think I'll send Marcus an email and remind him of that piece of his own story. It's a great example of the fact that having a mentality of **ABUNDANCE** takes away the fear that you won't have enough."

Sandy nodded. "It's so common to think, 'Will I have enough energy, or money, or people to help, or whatever I'll need?' rather than having faith that what's really needed will be provided if we're open to it."

Ross smiled. "Of course," he said, "you and I need to have that faith that we'll be able to pay Moving Mentor's fees, as well."

Sandy agreed. "It's really an investment in Mom and Dad's future well-being. Maybe they will even discover a new life ahead."

Moving Mentor's Journal

It's amazing how as people move whole-heartedly into this process, doors open and they begin to look at the future. My friend and client Roger expressed this idea in memorable terms when he told me, "I've been a husband, a father and a son. Now at 76 I'm going to find out who Roger is."

CHAPTER SEVEN

Making A Connection

Moving Mentor was careful to keep track with Sandy of any and all progress in working with her parents. During one of Sandy's phone calls to her friend Diane, the two decided to meet for lunch. Sandy was excited as she told Diane about her work with Moving Mentor.

"The most amazing time was last week when I was at my folks.'" Sandy said. "Moving Mentor and I had planned the whole thing out so it wouldn't be threatening to my dad. I'd brought my speaker phone with me, and when I mentioned to my mom that I'd set up a conference call with Moving Mentor she perked up. 'That's the person who helped Margie Gilbert make such a smooth move!' she said. Luckily my dad was in a good mood, kidding around a lot. I asked them if I could call Moving Mentor and have the four of us talk for a while, and he said okay."

"Hello there!" Moving Mentor's warm friendly voice came over the phone speaker. "I am so glad to meet you, Mr. and Mrs. Alverson. Sandy and I have been having some good talks, and I've been looking forward to talking with you folks as well."

"You have an interesting name," Everett Alverson said in a mischievous tone. "How many mentors have you moved lately?"

A hearty chuckle, and the voice came right back. "Just one, I'm afraid. I understand you were in the hardware business, Mr. A. My dad was a hardware wholesaler. Maybe you heard of his company, Sylvester and Moore. My dad was William . . . "

"You're Bill Sylvester's kid?" Everett's tone was more respectful. "Sure, I used to order from them a lot. How come he didn't take you into the business?"

"We actually talked about that. But then he died, and I ended up helping my mom."

"I have a friend, Margie Gilbert, who used your service," Lucille commented. "She was so delighted—"

"Hey," Everett interrupted. "I feel sorta like it's three to one here. Just when does this railroad station close?"

"Nobody's railroading you," Moving Mentor put in. "This call is for me to hear from the two of you about your situation, and to explore how I might be of help to you. Is that okay?"

Lucille smiled. Everett nodded. Sandy said, "Looks like a go."

"Good. First of all, you, Mr. and Mrs. Alverson, are in charge here. I know Sandy has talked with you about moving, but you may very well find that staying in your home is just right for you. Educating yourself about your options is the best thing you can do now. The goal is to maximize your independence and give you the best quality of life."

"I'll tell you what would maximize my independence about now," Everett huffed. "A new pair of legs so I can throw this damn walker away!"

"Maybe you need an armchair fitness program," Moving Mentor replied.

"What's that?" Everett growled.

"It's an exercise program that's all the rage these days. You'll have to visit a retirement center to learn about it, though."

"You mean a feeble farm?" Everett scoffed. "We've got one close by here. What's it called, Lucy? Aging Acres, or Senility City or something?"

"Maybe you want to buy a small ranch house," said Moving Mentor, undaunted. "Or a condo on one level. Maybe you could look at a place near Sandy, or modify the house you have now. What I'm saying is, it makes sense to look around. That way you are taking charge of change, rather than having it just happen to you. In the meantime, ask a real estate agent to come in and assess your place."

"I'm ahead of you there," Everett said proudly. "I've got a fellow bringing me comparables in a few days, and a ballpark figure of what this place is worth."

"Good for you. Let me know if I can help in any way."

"So," Sandy told Diane as she finished her tale, "the call was a success. My folks met Moving Mentor, and they liked her."

Sandy was again at Moving Mentor's website. She had learned to visit it often, for it was frequently updated. This time she found the heading "Three Key Principles for Helping Elders Move," which corroborated much of what she was learning as she worked with Lucille and Everett.

3 KEY PRINCIPLES FOR HELPING ELDERS MOVE

1. **Don't take it personally.**

   Remember the feelings seniors often associate with moving / downsizing:

   Loss—loss of independence, loss of control over their lives, loss of respect from self and others for taking help

   Fear—fear of loneliness, fear of isolation from family and friends, fear of the unknown

   Worries—over health, over money

2. **Listen.** When an elder needs to vent or emote

   <u>Avoid interference</u>—questioning, advising, reassuring

   Instead, <u>reflect</u> the feelings you hear or observe.

3. **Help them reframe.**

   Reframing is shifting the way you see a thing without changing the external situation at all, so that your feelings and responses toward it are placed within a different frame of reference.

<u>FROM</u>	<u>TO</u>
• Fear, clinging and worry	• Confidence, anticipation
• Loss	• Gain
• Maintaining false independence	• Enjoying healthy interdependence
• *I'm being put away*	• *A new life is opening for me.*

CHAPTER EIGHT

Life is What Happens

S low down, Everett. You're driving too fast. Besides, this isn't the shortest way there!"

Lucille Alverson was doing her usual backseat driving and—also as usual—her warning fell on deaf ears. As they pulled into a gas station, Everett's eyes were on the sign showing the latest gasoline price increase. There was a grinding screech of metal. Everett had sideswiped the car at the next pump! Asking his wife to take the registration from the glove compartment, he got out to talk with the irate driver. Then he noticed Lucille hadn't followed him. He looked back to find her beating on the inside of the damaged door. It couldn't be opened.

After the damage was assessed by the insurance company, a call from their agent brought bad news. "I'm sorry, Mr. Alverson, your accident places you in a new category. Your rates will be raised considerably unless you agree to attend an eight-week Safe Driving for Seniors class."

Everett erupted in anger and hung up. He called his son Marcus. "Who do they think they're talkin' to?" he foamed.

As he listened to his father's ranting, Marcus thought, *Maybe all Sandy's talk about Mom and Dad's situation is more on target than I thought.*

———•—•———

A certain feeling in the air announced that fall was ending, and soon the snow would fly. On a crisp morning Sandy's mother called her to say they'd spent the night at their neighbor's house. The furnace had quit again, and this time the neighbor couldn't fix it. Lucille's voice was despairing as she said, "We're going to have to put in a whole new furnace."

Sandy listened for a long time and as she hung up she sighed. "Wow," she said to herself, "they say life is what happens when you're making other plans, but enough is too much." She dialed the number for Maplewood Village and made an appointment to meet with the marketing director.

On her next visit to Moving Mentor's website, Sandy noted a change. An article was featured, entitled "Aging In Place— Wave of the Future?" She quickly linked to the reading:

Studies show that 85 percent of Americans would prefer to stay at home when reaching retirement age and beyond. A movement gathering force is offering seniors some new options, which add up to their continuing to live at home, while taking advantage of many of the services offered in a retirement community. An organization called StayAtHome compiles and evaluates services from snow shoveling to nursing care, then puts members in touch with them. It also negotiates group discounts for some services.

Suppose your aging parents need home-making services, or someone to make dinner, vacuum the floor or change linens. If they belong to StayAtHome, they can call the organization's director, who would link them to the needed service, one which StayAtHome has thoroughly screened.

The point of the organization is to serve as a middle man between the private person who is looking for services and the commercial providers. The beauty of it is that you can stay in your home and have coordination services if you need them. You have a director who finds whatever you need, whether it's a ride to the doctor or someone to clean your gutters. Perhaps the assisted living communities, as well as facilities for more active seniors, have new competition. The possibilities for stay-at-home clients seem endless. Such services as catered meals several times a week, home safety assessments, gourmet cooking clubs and "friendly callers" to check on seniors would break isolation, providing a kind of return to the days when most people's extended families lived close by and could assist them in their old age.

Another plan gathering interest was started by a group of four senior couples who together dedicated themselves to helping each other. Each pair planned their living spaces and needs, and identified their skills and strengths that could be used in the communal living venture. Then they looked around and found a large multi-family home that would meet their needs, and pooled their resources to purchase it. The project is going well, and other groups are studying it.

Sandy wondered if such an option could work for her parents. She decided to find out whether either of these movements was under way in their area.

The last conference call between Lucille and Everett's offspring had closed with tensions high all around. Since then, Ross had emailed Marcus his reminder to "think abundantly."

Jeff had done his financial homework. "I called Crosby who appraised their house, and he told me we're in the ball park. Mom and Dad could sell the house and have enough for a good down payment on another place. Or, they could get a reverse mortgage."

"What's that?" Sandy asked.

"It's like an equity line of credit, except the bank pays an agreed-upon fixed amount monthly to the home owner to provide extra income." As Sandy considered this, Jeff added, "There are two other issues we need to raise with the folks. One is power of attorney and the other is a health care proxy." Jeff went on to explain and discuss these two important matters. When Sandy hung up she felt grateful; it meant so much to have Jeff taking this active role.

⸰⸰⸰

"Honey, look at this," said Lucille. She held out to Everett the feature story of the home and garden section of the Sunday paper. "See what the headline says? House prices may have reached their peak." Then she gasped as she looked at his ashen face. "Darling, are you all right?"

Everett's eyes rolled back and he mumbled some incoherent phrases. Lucille ran for the phone and dialed 911. All her thoughts about the housing situation were abandoned as a cold dread crept over her heart. "Oh God, Oh God please!" she pleaded.

The ride in the ambulance seemed interminable. The wait at the hospital was even longer.

When Lucille tried Sandy, first at home and then on her cell phone, she couldn't reach her. She slumped into a chair in the waiting room, her mind in a whirl. Soon she dozed, utterly exhausted.

"Mrs. Alverson?"

She woke with a start. "Yes," she replied.

"I'm Dr. Spellman. Your husband is resting comfortably now and he is stable. We are going to keep him for observation. It seems he has had a cerebral incident, something like a tiny stroke. You may see him now for a few minutes."

A few days later, Lucille came home after visiting Everett who was now in a rehab facility and who was doing better each day. As she entered the house, a door knob that had been loose came off in her hand. When she went to Everett's basement workshop to get tools to fix it, she threw up her hands. "What an abominable clutter!" Returning with a screwdriver and wrench, she saw they did not fit. *I don't even know how to use them, anyway.* She threw the tools aside in frustration.

During those days when she wasn't visiting Everett, Lucille kept herself busy. But often in her mind desperate thoughts loomed. *What if I were to lose Everett? I'd be trapped in this old house. What if I died, and he were still living here, helpless?* Lying in bed in the dark at night, she was unnerved by little noises in the house.

One morning Lucille looked out her window to see that a heavy snow had fallen during the night. How would she get the driveway cleared? *Another thing Everett always saw to.* After calling a friend for the name of a young man who had a snowplowing business she waited all day, but he failed to show up. Late in the afternoon she called Everett to say she wouldn't be visiting him today. She made sure she wasn't crying during the time she talked to him.

Lucille had other concerns. It made her nervous to drive the unfamiliar rental car to see her husband; at the same time she thought, *I don't want Ev to see how upset I am.* During their visits he often complained about the facility he was in, calling the care he received "unnecessary fussing." Plainly, he wanted to come home.

On Thursday as Lucille was leaving to drive home, the doctor told her that Everett would be coming home in a few days. She sighed as she went to the parking lot. Everett's return would be both a relief and a new set of worries.

———•◦•———

"Hello? Is this Moving Mentor?"

"Yes it is. Who's calling, please?"

"It's Lucille Alverson. We had a conference call a few weeks back."

"Oh, yes, Mrs. Alverson. Sandy's told me of your husband's episode. I understand he's coming home tomorrow."

"That's why I'm calling." For the next minutes, a torrent of fears and concerns poured out of Lucille.

Moving Mentor listened. Finally she said, "I understand. Naturally you are concerned. You can't see what's ahead. You can't plan anything."

"That's exactly right."

"I'm going to share something with you." Moving Mentor paused meaningfully. "When you need to move forward, but aren't sure where the path is leading, it helps to have a **LANTERN** at your feet."

"What do you mean?"

"I think Sandy may have told me you were raised in the country?"

"Yes. I'm a farm girl."

"Back then, weren't there some dark nights when you had to go out to do some chores, and you carried a lantern?"

"Oh yes, often."

"Do you remember how, walking with that lantern through the dark, it lighted up just enough of the path ahead for you to take the next step? You weren't afraid because, even though you couldn't see far ahead, you could see where to take that next step. And that was enough."

It had been years since Lucille had thought about these things. Now, as she sensed where this was leading, tears came to her eyes.

"That's the way," Moving Mentor went on, "that you experience certain times in this process you're going through. You only have the light to see the next step you need to take. And that is enough."

———•◦•———

Moving Mentor's Journal

The Alversons are so lucky. Embedded in the way things have been set up here are opportunities for them to say the things that are in their hearts and be with one another in ways that really matter.

It's ironic to be dealing with people about the mechanics of moving to a new place, when all the while the reality lies beneath. They're all engaging in a journey they knew they would have to take, but have gotten good at avoiding. It's not a journey towards death, but toward finding the essence of life.

I'm the one that needs to remember that the move is the vehicle for doing the work of a lifetime. I can only facilitate, but they get to decide where to let this take them.

The next morning Lucille left a voice message for Sandy. "I'm resolved to make my life simpler. Please come and help me." About noon she was surprised to get a call from her oldest son. "Guess what, Mom," Marcus said. "I'm making a trip to Boston today, and I'll stop by overnight to see you. How about I come by the house and pick you up so we can visit Dad at the rehab together?"

"Is Julia coming with you?"

"No, I'll be alone."

As he hung up his cell phone, Marcus thought about his wife. *Thank goodness Julia's not going with me. Seeing Mom and Dad without her is easier. All these years and she doesn't get along any better with them than she did at the beginning.* As he thought about meeting with his father, Marcus was glad his mother would be there to act as a buffer.

When Lucille answered the door, Marcus said, "Are you ready to go, Mom?"

"I'll be ready in a few minutes. Meanwhile, I'd like you to see if you can fix this doorknob."

Marcus sighed quietly and resigned himself to the task. Descending into the basement gloom, he almost tripped on the stairs, which were stacked with piles of junk. It took him a while hunting through the jumble of tools and parts on Everett's work bench to find what he needed. In the process his eye caught an old shoeshine box he had made as a youngster. He picked it up and for a brief moment he was that boy again, surprising his dad with this gift.

Finding the tools he needed to help Lucille, he went upstairs thinking, *Was it always this messy when I was a kid? I remember working down here on projects, and things were in place where I could find them. Times have really changed.* Then he thought, *Many times I've thought we should just get a dumpster in here and throw everything in it. But then what would have happened to my shoeshine box?*

———•-•-•———

Moving Mentor's Journal

A dumpster is a handy thing, but certain of my experiences when I've been downsizing or packing clients have prejudiced me against that proverbial easy-out for adult children who are in a hurry to dispose of a household.

Last week I found a diary in John's attic. It had belonged to his first wife who died when their daughter Rachel was three. Today I put that diary in Rachel's hands. Now, at 46, she is connecting in a new way with the mother she hardly knew.

CHAPTER NINE

The Upside of Downsizing

Sandy hung up the phone after a long talk with her mother. She slumped onto the couch with her face in her hands.

"What's wrong, hon?" Ross asked.

"A million things. I'm worried about my mother, who's worried about my father. I've got a desk piled high with things to be done. We haven't had a decent family meal in I don't know how long. And I've been ignoring you."

Ross sat down and patted her arm. "Sounds like you think you don't have a life any more," he said.

Sandy sighed. "I'm a poster girl for the Sandwich Generation!"

"Okay, let's talk about what can be done to restore some balance to your life."

Sandy thought a while. "For one thing," she said, "I'm supposed to go to Mom's Tuesday to help her downsize some of her kitchen stuff. Maybe I could assign her some homework tasks in the meantime."

"That would take some of the pressure off you?"

"Right. Also, I've been thinking I could call Aunt May to come and stay with Mom and Dad for a few days. That would give me a chunk of time I need to catch up."

"Good," said Ross. "And I want you to give me some dates in the next two weeks so I can reserve us a couple of nights at Roswell's B&B."

Sandy's features lighted up, momentarily dispelling the careworn look. "That would be *fabulous*!" she exclaimed. "Maybe I *do* have a life of my own, after all!" While they hugged, Sandy said, "As long as we're talking, I've got something to confess."

"Oh no!" Ross said playfully. "You haven't been neglecting some important way of caring for us all, have you?"

Sandy smiled, then looked serious. "It's about a strange whispering I hear in the back of my mind these days. It says, *If I do this job of caring for my parents right now, maybe some day . . .* "

She paused, and Ross finished, "When your kids are your age, they'll take care of *you* that way."

Sandy nodded ruefully. "Pretty crazy, huh? They'll probably be on the other side of the world by then!"

———•◦•———

Driving to Westbrook a few days later, Sandy went over in her mind the principles Moving Mentor had shared with her about helping with the organizing of her parents' possessions.

> *Your parents are part of a generation that worked hard to acquire what they have. Everything was precious and reflected the sweat of their brow. They lived at a time when the rule was, Waste not, want not. You will find a kitchen drawer with a rubber-band collection, chuckle to yourself and remember the discipline with which that generation lived. All you can do is admire it.*
>
> *Going through possessions with your mother will be like an archeological dig. It will need to be done in layers. During the first session, and perhaps for many sessions after that, you will be helping your mother separate out the things she clearly no longer needs or wants. This applies even if she doesn't know whether she is moving. People will say to me,' I will only know what I want to keep when I know where I'm moving to.' And I say,' Don't worry about what you will keep. Worry about what*

you already know you <u>won't</u> keep—what you haven't used for ages and aren't likely to use again.'

There are three objectives here. The first has to do with creating room for new life in your mother's life. A cluttered house is like a cup that is filled to the brim. Until you empty some of the old out of it, there is no room for new. Taking away things your mom no longer uses will give her renewed energy.

The second objective is to make your mother's life simpler by having her keep only the things she still uses. If you can't remember where you put something—or, if it's so inaccessible you'd rather not bother to dig it out—what's the point of hanging on to it?

The third objective is to use the process of downsizing as a vehicle for spending precious time together.

———·•·———

Lucille was glad to see her daughter walk through the door. She watched as Sandy went to where Everett was watching a basketball game on TV, and hugged him. Then the women moved to the kitchen

"Let's sit down and have some tea, Mom, while we figure out how we'll work together," Sandy said.

After some catching up, she stood up. "Are you ready to start, Mom? You can sit here and be the armchair director while I bring things out of these lower cupboards for you to look at."

Shortly into the process Sandy thought, *Some things clearly have only one place to go. The trash.* She went to the garage and chose a large box from the pile there.

An hour later, the two women stopped and looked at what they had accomplished. The shelves were marked with removable colored stickers. Those marked with a red sticker were for items to be given away or sold. The yellow-marked shelves had items that Lucille couldn't make up her mind about. Shelves with green stickers held the items she was clear she was keeping.

Sandy had thought about packing up all the items to be given away, but in their discussion she and her mother decided that on his next visit Ross could bring his digital camera and take pictures of the items Lucille was not keeping. They could then send them out to the newlyweds, as well as to two of the grandchildren who were in the process of setting up homes of their own. Lucille loved this idea.

The next hour went by even more smoothly than the first. "This is so much easier than I thought," Lucille enthused. "I can't believe what this is doing. It feels just like the time—" She stopped and smiled.

"What, Mom?" Sandy asked.

"Once I was driving someplace, and I couldn't seem to get anywhere. I didn't know why I was being held back until I realized I'd been driving with the emergency brake on. When I released it, the car just moved ahead again like it should. That's what it's feeling like today, getting rid of things that are holding my life back. I might even soon be feeling in charge of things again."

Sandy grinned. "Moving Mentor says, Clearing out makes room for new life. There is **ENERGY** at work in the universe. She says even when you take the first small steps toward downsizing, there's a release of that energy. That's what you're feeling, Mom. And I'm feeling it, too."

They sat there a while. Suddenly Sandy laughed. "Look, Mom," she said, pointing at the trash box. "Look at what you've been holding on to, that you can now kiss goodbye," The pair giggled as they reviewed the items: four old toaster oven racks, five plastic coffee filter holders from long-defunct coffee pots, three glass vases of various shapes and sizes from florist deliveries, and a seemingly endless collection of aluminum foil pans and plastic containers from take-out food orders.

This was the first genuine laugh Lucille Alverson had had in many a day. She had forgotten what it felt like. She stood up and motioned Sandy to her feet. Smiling, Lucille grabbed a potholder and placed it on her daughter's head. Next she spread an apron over Sandy's shoulders like a cape, and had her hold an eggbeater upright in her right hand. Then she stepped back and applauded. Sandy grinned. "What in the world --- ?"

"Behold the Diva of Downsizing!" Lucille chanted. The two dissolved in laughter. Just then Everett's shout sounded from the next room as he cheered on his team. Lucille's whole form suddenly drooped, and her face fell.

"What's wrong, Mom?" Sandy said.

"You and I get it," Lucille said in a mournful voice. "But how are we ever going to get your father involved in this? The whole basement, the upstairs study—not to mention the garage—are his domains. And to call him a packrat is an understatement."

Sandy thought, *Maybe there's a role for brother Marcus in this.*

"It sounds like you and your mom had fun," Moving Mentor said, when Sandy called to report on the downsizing project.

"We did," Sandy said. "And guess what. We came across my grandmother's old meat-grinder—and she was willing to give it away! We had a good laugh when she told me how when she was a little girl she used to watch her mom push meat into the grinder, and watch it come out looking like worms!"

"It's wonderful to hear those stories."

"I'll bet you've got a lot of them you could tell," Sandy said.

Moving Mentor chuckled. "You're right. For instance, once I was cleaning out the attic of an elderly gentleman, and his grandchildren were helping me. In the middle of our work Susie, a fourth-grader, let out a whoop. She had come across her grandfather's fourth-grade report card! It was fun watching her as she reviewed his grades and the remarks his teacher had written. She told him: "See, grandpa? You had trouble with math just like I do!"

Moving Mentor's Journal

People worry that if they were to make this move, it would be their last. If they give up all their stuff, their life will be over. They don't say it, but what they fear is that moving puts them one step closer to the grave. They never dream that moving can actually infuse them with new life, or that getting rid of possessions can lift a weight off their shoulders and give them more freedom.

I like to ask each client if they still have unfulfilled dreams. I remember Maria, who finally got to spend time playing and enjoying the piano that had sat silent in her house for thirty years. There's no time for dreaming when you're burdened with detritus from the past.

CHAPTER TEN

Worth Every Minute

When Lucille opened the trunk and saw the old family lace on top, she couldn't believe it was almost a year since she and Sandy had carefully placed it there in preparation for the move. The family was about to gather for a housewarming. Lucille had reserved the private dining room at Maplewood Village where she and Everett were now living. The contents of the trunk were to be the focal point for sharing at the celebration. Moving Mentor had suggested they save these items of family memorabilia to be looked at collectively by three generations, once the move was over and the couple were well settled.

Lucille closed the lid again as she heard Everett coming in the door, fresh from the meeting of the resident committee he chaired.

"We won," he said with a flourish, "We got the space."

"Oh, I'm so glad," Lucille exclaimed.

Everett was beaming. "Now we can get those things Marcus and I saved from the old basement out of storage, and start setting up the new workshop for the residents here. It'll be like being in the hardware business again!"

He hobbled over to a cabinet and put a CD on. Soon the crooner was singing: "Who-oo-oo stole my heart away? Who-oo-oo—?" When Lucille heard it, she straightened up with a smile.

"Come here, Lucy my love," Everett said in a seductive voice. "If you don't mind dancing with a guy with a cane, let's do a little steppin'."

Lucille was glad those run-up days to the move were behind her now. There had been the scouting of retirement communities located near each of the children. Of the four they visited, three had had long waiting lists. They'd been glad to find an earlier opening at this place, but despite her commitment to moving, Lucille had felt deeply the pangs of leaving the place where she and Everett had lived for so many years. There was no getting around the fact that it was an uprooting.

Moving Mentor's careful planning and guidance—her going over the floor plan of the new place and helping decide where furniture would be placed; her coaching Sandy in seeing to all the details of contacting and instructing the movers; her suggestion that at least one of the children be present during the actual move, and that Lucille and Everett make themselves comfortable for a couple of nights before the move at a friend's home—had eased the way.

Especially comforting was when Moving Mentor suggested that the four of them—Lucille, Everett, Sandy and herself— meet and do a tour of the old house just before the movers came. They told stories and reminisced, and before leaving for the last time, they read a poem that gave them encouragement.

In the days after the move, Lucille was delighted to find every last detail covered. It was as if the new place, though smaller, had captured the essence of their life-style. She saw why Moving Mentor had taken such pains to study the old place - its floor plan, traffic patterns, use of areas and furniture arrangement and to consult so thoroughly about their preferences.

Moving from room to room, Lucille was awed by the care that had been taken to make her and Everett feel at home. Her kitchen drawers and cabinets required no searching for items; all were where she had suggested they be placed. In the desk in the den the files were arranged neatly in order, and pictures hung just right. She recalled that on the day they moved she had entered the master suite to find hers and Everett's toothbrushes laid out on the bathroom counter, and the bed made and turned down.

— · ◦ · —

Now, as Lucille looked down the long festive table, filled with the family members of her three children, all laughing and enjoying the meal, her eyes sparkled with joy. It had been many years since they had gathered this way, and Everett had decided he should invoke an old tradition from his own family of origin. He stood and clinked a glass with a spoon for attention.

"It's time for everyone to think of something he or she is thankful for," he said. "We'll go around the table and share. I'll go first." Everyone was quiet, looking to the family patriarch. They had to wait a few moments, though; after his hearty introduction, Everett seemed to be having trouble finding his voice.

His eyes dimmed with tears, Everett finally spoke. "I'm thankful to be surrounded by those I love—and especially my dear Lucy--in a place that has all the feeling of home, a place that's become my new castle-without-the-hassle!"

When the laughter subsided, he added, looking fondly at Lucille, "I guess I thought my life was pretty much over, but it seems like it's beginning again." Everett sat down to cheers and clapping.

"You're next, Mom," Sandy said. As the room quieted and Lucille looked around the table at all the smiling faces, Sandy thought her mother looked like a benevolent queen, beaming graciously upon her loyal subjects.

"Well, it's just like a dream," Lucille said. "A dream come true. I never have been happier. Just to have you all here to share our new place, which we treasure so much. Looking back, all the times that seemed like so much effort now seem easy. We have all of you to thank for that."

The sharing continued, each person taking a turn. Jeff earned a few laughs when he said, "I'm grateful that Mom and Dad's move has made me the family curator. Thanks, folks, for all the extra boxes of your stuff I have stored in my basement, waiting for us to figure out what to do with them."

Van and Josephine, now married almost two years and expecting their first child, were thankful for furniture they had received when Lucy and Everett moved. Then it was Sandy's turn. She turned to her parents and said, "I can't be grateful enough to see you both so happy here. This is just the best!"

The group was surprised when an infrequent participant in family affairs signaled for attention. It was Julia, Marcus's wife. "I'm grateful for a change I've noticed in Marcus," she said. "He's becoming the husband and father we always knew he was, but hadn't seen for a while. I have no doubt that it was the role he played in this drama of helping you, Lucille and Everett, with your move, that brought this about." She paused to wipe her eyes, and the children looked at each other silently, awestruck at Aunt Julia's sharing this way.

"I've watched from afar as this saga unfolded, " she continued, "and I confess I've been critical and stand-offish. But coming here today and seeing how wonderfully you're settled in, I guess I'm feeling sorry for myself that I haven't had a part in it, too." She smiled warmly at Lucille. "I really hope we can be better friends and frequent visitors, now that you two are beginning your new life here." There was applause as Julia went over and was gathered in Lucille's arms.

Marcus was last in line. He reached under the table and held up the old shoeshine kit he'd found in his parents' basement. "I'm grateful that this got saved for me," he said. "It's a symbol for me, a *shining example* . . ." (he waited for people to chuckle at his pun) " . . . of a big learning in my life that's happened over these past months. I'll tell you about it a little later, but right now it's my privilege to introduce a guest of honor." With that, he turned toward the door and said, "Won't you come in, please?"

Moving Mentor stepped into the room, to warm applause. She beamed and said, "I'm so happy and grateful to have a part in this celebration. Marcus was kind to invite me. He and I have planned a little presentation. It requires the six grandchildren to take part. Will each of you young folks please come with me into the next room?"

A few minutes later the group trooped back into the dining room. Each child carried a sign with a single large letter on it. Moving Mentor explained, "Each of these signs holds a key to the success of the move we are celebrating. When our sign-holders explain what the letters mean, one of you is invited to share with us what its principle means to you."

The first to present was teen-aged Caroline, whose sign showed a big R. "R is for *Reframe*," she said. She read from a script pasted on the back of her card:

REFRAME
To reframe means to see things
in a different way.
Without changing the facts of
the situation, you infuse them
with new meaning.

Caroline looked up and said, "Does anyone have a comment?"

Jeff raised his hand. "From what your Grampop shared, I think he's reframed the whole idea of moving!" This brought laughter and nods from Everett.

Next, ten-year-old Jamie stepped up to display the letter N. "N is for *Nibble*," he said with a laugh. Then he read:

NIBBLE

Bolting food is not a healthy habit, and it reduces enjoyment of a meal. The same is true of making a move. Biting off more than you can chew is a sure way to become tired and discouraged. Each step should be savored, and lead logically to the next.
A good rule is: *Never do as much as you can.*

Sandy chose to comment. "That's my ticket," she said. "I'm a task-bolter. I always want to get it all done *now*. But with Moving Mentor's help, as this move has progressed I've begun to learn how to savor the moment." Sandy turned to Ross and added, "I want to keep practicing."

Ross drew smiles and murmurs when he looked mischievously at Sandy and said, "You're right, honey. It makes things so much more enjoyable when you live life one bite at a time!"

Twelve-year-old Cassie brought attention back to the cards when she showed her E. "E stands for *Esteem*," she said, and shared her caption:

ESTEEM

Esteem means you think enough of yourself to own up to the things that worry or frighten you, and have the courage to move forward anyway. It means to quit pretending that everything is fine and that you are just the way you always were. You start from where you really are and create a vision for the best that the future can be.

"Well," Lucille said, "I have a comment to make on that one. Many was the time, on this journey we've been on, that I've been frightened. But I knew that I, and my wonderful husband, were worth the effort it took, so somehow I kept on. I've seen what facing fear is about, and how it helps to summon up the courage to think enough of yourself and tell the truth about what you really feel."

Everett nodded vigorously and added, "She's getting good at that!"

In the pause that followed, it seemed to be someone's turn to step up with a sign, but no one moved. Finally Moving Mentor motioned to Josh. The gangly teen shuffled forward and held up his sign. "See this A?" he said, fixing his audience with a steely look. "It stands for *Abundance*. So listen up, people!"

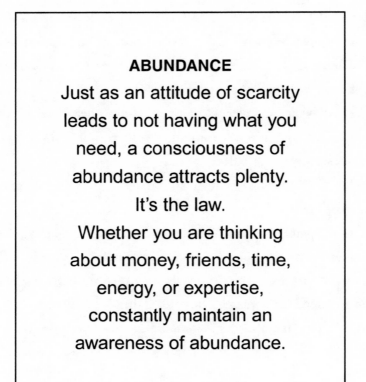

ABUNDANCE
Just as an attitude of scarcity
leads to not having what you
need, a consciousness of
abundance attracts plenty.
It's the law.
Whether you are thinking
about money, friends, time,
energy, or expertise,
constantly maintain an
awareness of abundance.

Marcus raised his hand to comment. "Some of you may know that I tend to be, well, somewhat conservative when it comes to money." This brought some good-natured murmuring among the clan.

"However, like my sister I am not above sharing a critical life-lesson from this relocation project. I never thought I'd say this, but I am learning how to act as if *there is always more where that came from.*" Cheers broke out.

Maddy was Jeff and Gretchen's eight-year-old, and the smallest member of the cast. She stepped forward confidently, her face glowing with the enthusiasm of a born actress, and pronounced, "L is for *Lantern*."

LANTERN

When you're not sure of
the way, think of how a lantern
lights the next step.

Maddy didn't wait for someone else to make the application. "I learned about this at camp," she said. "When I had to get up at night and go to the outhouse, I carried a lantern. It was scary, but I could always see the way." She bowed and curtsied as people applauded.

Amber, one of the married "children," was next with her E sign. "E stands for *Energy*," she told the group. Then she read:

ENERGY
The principle that "cleaning
out makes room for new life"
works because of the
renewing of energy it brings.

Marcus was last to come forward with a placard; his had a big W on the front. "At this time," he said, "we'd like Moving Mentor to please come up here." As the consultant made her way to the front, Marcus said, "We all agree that you, your wit and your wisdom were the keys to making my parents' move a healthy and happy one for us all." Applause rang out as he handed the consultant a small gift-wrapped box. "This is just a token, something to say 'thank you' from all of us."

Moving Mentor unwrapped the gift and held up a shining object. "It's a lovely pin," she said, "a pair of silver wings."

Marcus said, "That's because you, Moving Mentor, have appeared in our lives at just the right moment, and guided us through a difficult process. You've brought us comfort, support and practical wisdom. So W is for *Wings*—the wings of our angel!"

WINGS

In show-business language, an "angel" is someone who steps in and sees to it that a stage production is ensured of opening. It certainly helps to have an "angel" when you go through the big production of relocating. Having someone whose know-how and experience will help you plan ahead and make it through the rough spots is a God-send.

Now came the finale. On a signal from Moving Mentor, the seven sign-holders, who had stood holding their cards in the order they had presented, silently moved about to rearrange their order. Finally, there they stood with their letters spelling out the word

RENEWAL

'When you put all the pieces of a healthy relocation together," Moving Mentor said, smiling, "it adds up to RENEWAL for everybody who is fortunate enough to be involved."

———•—•———

Later, as the family members were moving out over the grounds of their loved ones' new community, Sandy went up to Marcus and gave him a hug. "I'm very proud of my big brother," she said. "Want to know why?" Marcus nodded sheepishly. "Because despite the feelings he grew up with of being short-changed by a father who was too busy to pay attention, he has willingly given back what he thought he didn't get, and helped to bring our family together in a whole new way."

———•—•———

The house-warming celebration was ending. Finally it was time for Moving Mentor and Sandy to say goodbye. After a long hug, the consultant handed her client a booklet. "I didn't tell you before," she said, "but during our work together, I've been compiling a Planning Guide for people like yourself who are faced with relocating their aging parents. I'd like you to have the first copy."

Sandy smiled as she read the title: *101 Ways to Get Your Parents Moving*. Leafing through the booklet, she exclaimed, "Why, it's all those steps you took me through—and more! This will be a help to so many people of my generation and their families. I'm honored to have it! And I hope you know it goes without saying that I could never have done this move without you. Thank you so much!"

Moving Mentor smiled. "Many people move, but not everyone *moves on*. Watching you grow throughout this time has been an inspiration to me."

Sandy smiled. "All this time I was thinking it was just Mom and Dad who were moving. It was also me! In fact, it was all of us."

———————

Moving Mentor's Journal

Now that the Alversons are in, I'm thinking again that when a move like this is finished, the outside is a reflection of the inner and the outer work that's been done. People think it's a place they're searching for, but when they're at ease because they've done their highest and best, they find that place inside themselves.

101 Ways To Get Your Parents Moving

*A Workbook for Helping
Aging Parents Downsize or Move*

by
Moving Mentor

*Dedicated to
all the Sandys
in the world*

For Adult Children Only

Introduction

Late one evening the phone rings in my home office. It's an adult daughter who lives half way around the world and who is home in the U.S. visiting her aging mother. She is shocked to find how fragile and forgetful her parent is compared to when she last saw her. Should she try to get her mother to move? Get help in the house? Another day an adult son in California calls to tell me his father on the East Coast has fallen and broken his shoulder. He is in for a long recovery and needs to be moved from his apartment to an assisted living facility. How can the son accomplish this, given his busy work schedule as an executive and the responsibilities of a growing family?

These days what to do about our aging parents is a hot topic. Much of the talk focuses on how baby boomers can deal with the need to relocate their parents. Some adult children will be hit by a crisis before they can do any advance planning. Others will have more time, which they can use to get the jump on what might otherwise become a disruptive and complicated situation.

What is your situation? Have you put off dealing with this time bomb? Maybe you've tried to broach the subject with your parents and have been rebuffed. Maybe you've put in token visiting time without any systematic plan. Or maybe you've just spent time worrying. There are definite ways to prepare yourself and your parents for what is ahead. By making sound decisions now, you and your parents can hold on to the best of the past—and create a quality future. You can actually add life by the choices you make now.

Taking Charge Gently

As adult children who contemplate initiating a conversation with our parents about their relocating, we do well to walk a mile in their shoes. They're not called the GI Generation for nothing. Having grown up in uncertain times and with fewer means, they are used to soldiering through and making do with the way things are. "Home" to them is likely to be the symbol of all they have accomplished, so to think of leaving it may even challenge their self-respect. In their thinking, the subject of finances may always have been off-limits to their children. Even if they have money, these stalwarts have been saving it for so long for a rainy day they don't recognize the rain when it comes. (If the mortgage is paid off, why would they dream of an outlay of expense?)

All our lives we've seen our parents as strong and self-reliant. They went through a war, they built a peace, and they resent intrusions into the solidity and predictability they've maintained for decades. They're holding on for dear life to the old ways of doing things, but many of those ways no longer serve. We've taken it for granted they would have seen this coming, made a plan, provided financially for it, etc. But their lives have not equipped them, as ours have us, to handle change.

Asking for help is not part of their vocabulary, either. Even if they've done some thinking and planning, they are still fearful and alarmed and most don't have the tools to communicate about it. Unaccustomed to feeling-talk, they're hesitant to share their grief over leaving the storied homestead. It's up to us, the members of the Emotionally Outspoken Generation, to take gentle charge.

Handling Difficult Situations

Sometimes difficulties get in the way of progress. For example, your parents may not agree with each other about moving (one wants to move, one doesn't; they want different places, etc.). You can start working on downsizing with the willing parent, get a realtor in, or work on home repairs.

A second challenge might be when siblings have gone their separate ways. If you and your siblings don't get along, you might choose to visit and work with your parents at different times. Or take on different roles: while one handles finances, another organizes or handles legal matters while a third, handy with the internet, manages sales of possessions through eBay. Team members need not talk a lot; they can report progress to each other through e-mail. (In one instance where siblings didn't have the time, energy, or inclination, parents hired a senior move manager*, and all communication was through that person.)

Looking in the Mirror

Raising the topic of moving Mom and/or Dad is likely to stir a host of family dynamics. If the home your parents are rattling around in is the one you grew up in, the place is furnished with memorabilia, rife with stories, peopled by good and bad ghosts of the past. In taking on helping your parents move, you may find yourself confronted both with the task of the letting-go of your own childhood and your own aging.

Planning ahead for spending increased time managing your parents' affairs requires you to rethink the way you manage things in your own life. If you have time before such conditions engulf you, use it to make changes. De-cluttering your own house creates energy for your parents to move on. It makes room for you to take items from your parents' home (even some you don't want). If your parents' situation is stable enough,

---

* *Senior move managers can facilitate every aspect of the moving process, from communicating with family members to helping people make decisions about what they'll keep, to supervising moves. If you think your parents need this help because you can't be there or can help only intermittently, contact www. nasmm.org, website of the National Association of Senior Move Managers.*

you can put things into place or rearrange aspects of your own life in anticipation of their needing more support from you. Check out your employer's family-leave policy, or start saving vacation time. Make sure your own legal and financial affairs are in order. If you own your own business, you can take on more help so you can be out of town, managing this ongoing project of parenting your parents.

There's an agreeable-sounding myth that says your parents will go to some community and have all the care they need, and you can go back to life-as-usual. The fact is, there is no life-as-usual, at least not in the way it was before the moving process began. Inevitably, new things will come up—financial matters, processing visits with doctors which their community is not equipped to handle, etc. Your timely involvement now in their situation enables you to grow into this new role, and gives your parents time to accept it.

Building a Bridge to A New Life

Most people think the subject of moving aging parents starts with deciding where they will live. This is important, but it's usually a premature consideration. You can get things started by going through what is in the present home and making plans for what will happen to it. You'll notice that in shifting things that have long been stationary, the energy of life starts to move and doors to new thinking open up. It's as if you've dislodged one piece of a logjam.

It may be difficult, even painful, but by communicating about this topic with our parents we may be opening up a rich opportunity in our own lives. We have the potential not only to heal old wounds but also to revitalize family relationships. Despite daunting challenges, we need to acknowledge that a very narrow window remains for us to appreciate what our parents' generation has brought into the world. People their age are dying at the rate of a thousand a day. Now that we're to inherit the world in earnest, we need no longer resist spending time in that culture and in our parents' homes, the way we may have, growing up. We can appreciate their history and heal old wounds.

A letter received from a client says it best:

> I'm an only child, but my mother and I never got along. Growing up in her home was difficult, and I couldn't wait to move away. Yet since my father's death four years ago I've been managing my mom's affairs long-distance. I tried to keep her in her own home, but things got too complicated. Last year you helped her move, and nine months later, as you know, she was diagnosed with a

terminal illness. I took two months of family leave to help care for her at the close of her life. You helped me clean her cottage. By the time it was done, all the i's were dotted and the t's were crossed. Now, having done all there was to do, I can live the rest of my life with an inner peace. It's great to think that I was given a chance to do it right, the second time around.

101 Way to Get Your
Parents Moving

This booklet is designed as a tool for helping you coach and support a loved one throughout the process of moving. Whether you are an adult child, a friend or a relative, you can use it as a guide to facilitate an elder who is downsizing and/or relocating.

Who Does What?

Moving is a developmental process. The goal is to create a state of readiness both physically and psychologically. The division of roles in this process is anything but straightforward and clear-cut. It plays out much like a dance; each partner contributes to the readiness for taking the next step. Don't be alarmed at apparent stops in the forward movement of things. For instance, your parents may invite you to help them, then reject your aid as soon as it is given.

It's useful to think of a move as occurring in fairly predictable stages, each of which has its appropriate tasks that will build a bridge to a new life. This booklet divides 101 tasks into eight groupings, each of which represents a stage in the moving process. While the stages we have developed are markers along the way, the exact order of the tasks is not important. The steps themselves create the readiness necessary to complete the process.

We are using the convention of describing each task from the senior's point of view, but any one of these tasks could be handled by an adult child or a loving relative or friend. You and your parents will continually be making decisions about who does what. You may be facilitating the stages by reminding them to take the steps or by being with them as they carry them out—or doing them yourself, or delegating them to someone else.

Another invaluable resource—especially if you are working alone or are an only child—is a senior move manager. The numbers and availability of these professionals are increasing, and they can be life-savers.

Stages of the Move

STAGE 1
WORKING BEHIND THE SCENES

*At this stage your parents might
be saying, "The only way I'm
ever moving from here is when
they carry me out feet first!"*

Your parents have been living in their home for a long time, and are set on staying there. While they are not ready to talk about moving, and resist any mention of it, there are still steps you can take.

1) Create a book of memories about your home and your life there, or buy a ready-made book which you can fill in. Include special family times, holiday events, amusing anecdotes, etc.

2) Take pictures of each room in your home. Make a photo album.

3) Contact family members and ask them to come and collect anything in the house belonging to them. Set a deadline for removal.

4) Identify five things you don't use, want or need any more, to give away or throw away. The kitchen is a good place to start.

5) Call local charities (such as Goodwill, Salvation Army, Big Brothers and Sisters, Survival Center, Hospice, or schools, libraries or hospitals) and

inquire about their donation policies. Do they pick up? Do they want items on hangers or in bags, etc. Sometimes local colleges can use photography equipment, computers, etc.

6)   Clean out a drawer or closet.

7)   Contact your financial advisor, accountant, or attorney for advice on current tax and other information that is pertinent to staying in your home or selling it.

8)   Write a mission statement to carry you into the future. Make it simple and uplifting. Have it express how you will use your gifts and talents as you move ahead in your life. Think of a dream you had when you were younger, that you could still fulfill.

STAGE 2
GATHERING INFORMATION

*At this stage your parents might
be saying, "Maybe we can!"*

Your parents are willing to talk about moving. You are helping them look around the house, make inquiries, and gather information.

9) Talk with your spouse, a friend or a family member about what a move might mean to you. Identify your needs; list and rank-order them.

10) Think about what kinds of living situations might suit you now. Make inquiries about potential places to live. Arrange to visit several of them. If appropriate, place your name on some waiting lists.

11) Consult with your accountant or a financial advisor about the affordability of different options you are considering.

12) Make a list of needed repairs inside your home. Arrange to have the work done.

13) Make a list of things to take care of on the outside of your home, including landscaping, painting and cement work.

14) Ask a few realtors to visit your home to give you an idea of its value, so if you decide to sell it you will have the information you need.

15) Begin removing items you no longer need or want, so your house will look its best if you decide to put it on the market.

16) Buy a package of *removable* stickers in assorted colors at your local stationery store or office supply store.

17) Identify possessions that are important for you to keep. Pick one color sticker and stick one on each of those items.

18) Ask friends, family, local real estate agents for the names of appraisers. Interview them by phone and select one to appraise items of yours that may be of value. (Ask about both insurance and replacement value.)

19) Think about and discuss what should happen to possessions you will not keep. Will you send them to auction? Will family/friends be taking them? Will they be donated? Will you hold a tag/estate sale? Consult with your accountant/ financial advisors about the options that will be best for you.

20) Look at real estate listings in local newspapers and other publications, as well as on the internet, to educate yourself about home sales.

STAGE 3
SORTING AND ORGANIZING

*At this stage your parents might be
saying, "I think I'm moving, but
I don't know where or when."*

It's becoming clear that your parents will be making a move, even though the time and place are unknown. Meanwhile, you can be busy seeing to important details that will smooth the way, once the destination is known. You are becoming more concrete about a plan, moving things around in the house, and making some decisions about possessions that are no longer needed.

21) Clear a space in your home in which you can work on downsizing tasks, packing, etc.

22) Clean out un-needed items from filing cabinets, paper file boxes, etc. This makes them easier to move.

23) Call your accountant and ask how long you need to keep tax documents, bank statements, financial records, etc.

24) Put legal documents and other important papers where you can easily find them.

25) Buy a shredder or arrange for the shredding of important papers you are discarding.

26) Make a plan for spending time on other important paperwork. (As the move gets closer, it becomes harder to concentrate on these tasks.)

27) Make an inventory of furniture you are hoping to move. Make the list room by room.

28) Call your waste management company for guidelines about what they will take at curbside and what needs to go to the landfill.

29) Inquire about the disposal of hazardous waste.

30) Go through your storage areas—attic, basement, closets, garage—and get rid of as many unwanted items as you can <u>now</u>. (This pays off when you put your house on the market, as the house will have to stay neat and tidy and you will have limited time for sorting and dispensing).

31) Ask family members to come and use colored stickers to designate items they'd like to have if you don't take them with you. (It is fine for items to have several different colored stickers on them, showing they have been tagged by more than one person.)

32) Collect packing materials—old newspapers, clean newsprint, boxes, labels, sealing tape, masking tape, see-through closeable bags in various sizes, bubble wrap, tote boxes, and lawn-and-leaf size trash bags with drawstrings.

33) Have the appraiser you selected appraise designated possessions.

34) Sort through your photos, scrapbooks and other memorabilia. Obtain plastic mildew-resistant bins to store the items you are going to keep. If time is short, plan to transfer these items to plastic bins now, but plan to sort them after the move when you are well settled.

35) Discuss with your realtor and other advisors the prose and cons of getting an independent home inspection. If you decide to get your home inspected, follow up on the inspector's recommendations.

STAGE 4
MAKING IT HAPPEN

*At this stage your parents
might be saying, "I hope I'm
doing the right thing!"*

Now your parents are committed to moving and making their lives simpler. They know where they are going, and they are anticipating the move. Much attention is going toward the new place and envisioning the new life as a reality. You and they are creating a bridge between the old and the new.

36) Make arrangements for placing your home on the market.

37) Make a list of affixed items (such as light fixtures) which you plan to take with you, so potential buyers will know what does and does not come with the house.

38) Be sensitive to how potential home buyers might view your home. Think about softened lighting, buying an air purifier, etc.

39) Contact your attorney and find out if he/she handles real estate transactions. Or, contact a real estate attorney.

40) Ask friends, neighbors and your realtor to recommend reputable movers. Develop a list of 3 movers to call.

41) Obtain a floor plan of your new home.

42) List items you will take, and items you may take if there is room. Make written notes of any existing marks, scratches or damages.

43) Measure large items and write their measurements on your furniture inventory list (see #27).

44) Walk through your new location with a tape measure, double-checking floor plan measurements. Measure windows and note locations of phone, electrical and cable outlets.

45) After measuring each room in your new place, check the inventory of things you are taking with you, to make sure of the fit. Using graph paper, create a floor plan of your new home. Make several copies, and experiment on paper with different furniture arrangements in each room.

46) Think about your new life-style before putting things back the way they've always been. Floor planning is not only about placing furniture so that it will fit; it's about using your new space creatively.

47) Ask a friend or family member to help you do a walk-through of your present home. Share stories about items and spaces that recall meaningful events.

48) Start cleaning out and sorting things into categories—what definitely goes with you, what definitely doesn't, and undecided.

49) As you sort, start packing up items in storage areas and closets. Begin with things you know you will not need until after you are settled in your new home.

50) As you pack boxes, label each box as to where it came from and where it should go in your new home.

51) Arrange for the new location to be cleaned.

52) Measure storage spaces in your new place, especially closets. Plan the use of these spaces carefully in advance.

53) Obtain proper shelving and arrange for work to be done in storage areas to maximize use of the space.

54) If appropriate, make arrangements for window treatments to be made or purchased.

STAGE 5
CREATING A TIME-TABLE

At this stage your parents might
be saying, "I feel like I've got
a foot in each place!"

Your parents are experiencing all the emotions of a big change, looking forward with anticipation and looking back with nostalgia. You are coordinating, strategizing, contacting helpers and agencies, doing preliminary packing, and overseeing many logistical details.

55) Call movers and ask preliminary questions. (How much advance notice do they need? How do they charge? Extra fees on weekends? Can they provide references? How do they wrap things? Do they move bureaus with contents inside? Do they insure items they do not pack themselves?

56) Arrange for 3 estimates. Be sure to tell movers in advance if you want help with packing.

57) Call your insurance company and review your policy. Ask about your coverage during the move. If your present home is not being sold right away, ask about continued coverage. Also, arrange for coverage in your new location.

58) Arrange with a storage facility to house items you plan to keep which will not fit into the new location. If you have items you're not sure

about keeping, store them temporarily until you decide.

59) If your move is local, plan to leave time to move most kitchen and bathroom items *before* moving day, if that is possible.

60) In your own mind, set a preliminary date for your move. Use a calendar to work backwards from that date to see if the timetable will work.

61) Pack on a room-by-room basis. Check each room for items you may have hidden over the years.

62) Send draperies and rugs to the cleaners, and arrange for furniture to be reupholstered in time to coordinate with your move.

63) If you decide to have any furnishings repaired, make arrangements so that the repaired pieces can be delivered to your new location around your scheduled moving date.

64) Make plans for proper care of your pets and plants.

65) As you plan the logistics for the move, think about your specific needs and how to care for yourself so as to ease the strains of relocating (for instance, it's easiest to set up your new kitchen before the actual moving date).

66) Think about whether you will stay in your home the night before and/or night after moving, or if staying elsewhere might work better for you.

STAGE 6
PACKING

At this stage your parents
might be saying, "Where did
I ever get so much stuff?"

You and your parents are fully engaged in getting everything into boxes. At the same time, you are readying the house for sale and making arrangements for where your parents will stay during the move and other ways to provide for them during the actual transition. The movers will soon be on the way.

67) Plan to have at least one companion with you during your move. Moving is too much to do alone.

68) Call movers as soon as you can to book your moving date.

69) Label each box according to number and/or destination. Label it on its top, and also on two sides. This way you can see the number or label from several angles when boxes are stacked (see #50).

70) Create a master list that itemizes your boxes. Use 4 columns labeled: *Box #, Contents, From, To.* This way, when boxes are carried into your new home it will be easy to see where they should go. Make notes in the margin of any nicks, cracks or other imperfections in items you are packing.

71) As you pack, use the master list to note what to unpack immediately and what to unpack later.

72) Pack liquor boxes with books and small heavy objects.

73) Pack heavier items on the bottom of boxes with lighter ones on top. Fill in all spaces with crumpled newsprint, towels or linens.

74) Wrap all dishes and breakable items separately with newsprint or towels. Use plenty of padding between items. Dishes should be packed sideways, not flat.

75) Pack hanging clothes in wardrobe boxes. (These may be rented or purchased from the moving company. They will also deliver them.)

76) Take frequent rests while packing.

77) Pack items to be donated in plastic leaf bags.

78) Make a list of all items to be donated and make copies of it. Arrange for items for donation to get to their destinations.

79) Keep a box open for things you'll want to go on the truck last, and be taken off first. Label "Last on, First off." (Examples: bedding, bath and kitchen essentials, pet food, telephone, TV remote control, tissues, toilet paper, shower

curtains, extension cords, extra TV cable
wire, paper plates, soap, nightlight, flashlight,
lightbulbs, garbage bags, tools, etc.)

80) Organize a first aid kit and tool kit; keep them
handy while you are packing and moving

81) Organize medications; keep enough medicine
with you to see you through the move.

82) Read your mover's Bill of Lading. Be sure you
understand the extent of your mover's liability
for loss and damage.

STAGE 7
AS MOVING DAY APPROACHES

At this stage your parents might be
saying, "This could be interesting!"

You're attending to many last-minute details. If the move is local, you've arranged to move the kitchen and bathroom items first, ahead of the rest of your parents' possessions. How would your parents like to say goodbye to their old home?

83) Think about phone service in your new home. Will you order new service? Will you use your old number at your new location? What about long distance service?

84) Obtain a change-of-address packet from your post office and fill it out. Send notifications to charge accounts, credit card companies, community organizations, social security office and IRS, as well as relatives and friends.

85) Make appropriate banking changes. If you are opening an account in another location, be sure there is enough in your present accounts for outstanding checks to clear.

86) Cancel or change newspaper deliveries.

87) Order change in cable service. If moving out of state, call the motor vehicle bureau in your new

location and obtain information about changing your auto registration.

88) Arrange for final reading of your electricity, water, and fuel meters.

89) Pick up dry cleaning or other items of yours that may be at local shops. If appropriate, remove items from your safe deposit box.

90) Consult with your insurance and moving company about coverage of your possessions during the move. If appropriate, buy additional coverage from the movers.

91) Check ahead as to what forms of payment are acceptable to your mover. Be prepared to pay at the end of moving day, if that is required. (Check your bank balance to be sure you have enough to cover more than the estimate.) Keep some cask on hand in case you wish to tip moving men.

92) If your mover permits items to travel in drawers, place loose items that are in dresser or desk drawers in clear plastic bags and replace them in the drawers. Fill drawers that are not full with towels or linens so contents cannot shift during the moving process.

93) Arrange for final clean-up in your old location, including spackling of holes in walls where picture hooks have been removed.

94) Provide movers with complete directions to your new location and give them a phone number at which they can reach you.

95) Put a pair of removable stickers or small tags on each lamp shade and lamp, and write the same letter on each. This will help in matching lamps and shades later. Also, note on a list which room each lamp comes from.

96) On moving day place bed linens in an empty drawer or box that will be accessible in the evening in your new home.

STAGE 8
AFTER THE MOVE

At this stage your parents might
be saying, "I never expected it
to have the feeling of home!"

It's a wrap. The movers have come and gone. You've done the address changes, and the phone and TV are working in the new place. All the planning was worth it.

97) Make sure the mover's inventory is correct. Go around your new home with the mover and make a note if you disagree with the condition of items on the inventory that were moved. Refer back to your home inventory or the notes you made of the conditions of items before the move.

98) Do not sign off on the mover's inventory until you have carefully inspected for damage. If you do find damage, save the boxes. Make sure all items packed by movers are unpacked. (You have a limited amount of time to report damages on items they packed.)

99) Make a written note of any missing boxes or damages, and call your moving company immediately.

100) For a reference to a new doctor, dentist and other health care professionals in your new location, ask your new neighbors and acquaintances

or call your insurance company. Have your medical records transferred. Do the same for your pets.

101) Do only essential unpacking on the first night. Consult your master list to locate boxes which are of primary importance. Then, take 24 hours or more to rest and celebrate.

About the Authors

Barbara Z. Perman, Ph.D., is founder and President of Moving Mentor, Inc., a company that provides moving management consulting and organizing services. Dr. Perman specializes in helping seniors and their families through the arduous tasks related to downsizing and relocating. As educator, speaker, coach, family consultant, professional organizer and author, she has written and developed books and products that support the moving process from beginning to end. Barbara holds a Masters degree from Oxford University and a Doctorate in Psychology from Edinburgh University in Scotland.

Jim Ballard is an established author of a number of books about managing change and transforming the people side of business. In addition to his own titles published by Random House, John Wiley and Beyond Words, Ballard has co-authored a number of books with best-selling author Ken Blanchard, published by Simon & Schuster, McGraw-Hill, Jossey-Bass and Harper-Collins.

Both authors are experienced keynote speakers, and both design and facilitate seminars and workshops. They are in demand as presenters to many different groups around the country.